SHADOWS IN THE SOIL
Human Bones & Archaeology

Ex umbris et imaginibus in veritatem

SHADOWS IN THE SOIL
Human Bones & Archaeology

TONY WALDRON

TEMPUS

First published 2001

PUBLISHED IN THE UNITED KINGDOM BY:

Tempus Publishing Ltd
The Mill, Brimscombe Port
Stroud, Gloucestershire GL5 2QG

PUBLISHED IN THE UNITED STATES OF AMERICA BY:

Arcadia Publishing Inc.
A division of Tempus Publishing Inc.
2 Cumberland Street
Charleston, SC 29401
1-888-313-2665

Tempus books are available in France, Germany and Belgium
from the following addresses:

Tempus Publishing Group	Tempus Publishing Group	Tempus Publishing Group
21 Avenue de la République	Gustav-Adolf-Straße 3	Place de L'Alma 4/5
37300 Joué-lès-Tours	99084 Erfurt	1200 Brussels
FRANCE	GERMANY	BELGIUM

British Library Cataloguing in Publication Data.
A catalogue record for this book is available from the British Library.

ISBN 0 7524 1488 7

Typesetting and origination by Tempus Publishing.
PRINTED AND BOUND IN GREAT BRITAIN

Contents

List of illustrations

List of tables

Preface

Shadows have form but little substance. Skeletons in the ground have human form but how much substance can be derived from them? To what extent can we reconstruct the lives of those whose remains we excavate and examine? The purpose of this book is to examine these questions and try to provide answers in what I hope is a readily accessible form. This is not a book for the specialist and I have not assumed that the reader will have much knowledge of anthropology, epidemiology or pathology and I have tried to keep the text as free of jargon as possible. Some of the opinions which are put forward here are controversial — a few, contentious — but I hope that they may act as an antithesis to some of the more extravagant claims made for the study of human remains in some quarters.

Studying human remains has given me much pleasure and the problems encountered have been challenging and I have enjoyed trying to solve a few of them. I am grateful to those friends and colleagues who have encouraged, educated, argued, disagreed, sometimes been convinced but always borne with me over the years.

Writing a book is like starting a new love affair; it is completely absorbing and the hapless author or lover can think of nothing else. I acknowledge my sins of omission to my family who have been neglected and who have not complained, even when notes and drafts seemed to cover every flat surface in the house. Without their love and support this book — and indeed much else — could not have been accomplished. They know how grateful I am to them all.

Tony Waldron
London 2000

Introduction

Interest in human remains has probably never been so great as at present. At the time of writing, there are at least four terrestrial television programmes which feature bones or bodies, while the satellite channels provide various aspects of forensic science in which bodily parts often feature prominently. And this at a time when death has been sanitised in our society — few people die at home now, and most of the population has never seen a dead body. Part of the interest in the dead from the past is certainly voyeuristic and one cannot altogether exclude some of one's colleagues from that accusation. But the greater part has to do with a sense of continuity. We do not have extended families anymore, grandparents are rarely on hand to describe how things were in the past or to provide information on other branches of our families, and it is perhaps to make good this deficiency — to satisfy our curiosity of where we have come from — that we take such an interest in those who lived many generations ago.

Archaeologists will attest to the crowds which may gather when skeletons are revealed on a site and will often have to provide guards on the site to prevent theft. Skulls are usually the most sought after of the remains and sometimes even find their way into antique shops for sale. I saw two human skulls in a shop in York but the shifty owner would not give me their provenance. A few years ago I went to see the vault on the leper island of Spinalonga near Crete. The jumbled remains of those who had died on the island were revealed by torchlight but our guide said the bones were being robbed by clandestine visitors to the island and that it was likely that the vault would soon have to be closed. Sure enough, returning again recently, the vault had been cemented over to prevent further desecration; the authorities quite properly thought that those buried there had suffered enough.

If skeletons attract public attention, this is nothing compared with the finding of a body with fleshy parts, or with the unwrapping and examination of a mummy. A mummy will get a CAT scan at the drop of a hat and certainly well before any living patient. The x-raying of mummies has a very venerable history — Grafton Elliot Smith was the first to x-ray a mummy in 1903 when he was professor of anatomy in Cairo. He was examining the royal mummies and stuck that of Thutmosis IV into a taxi for the journey round to the private clinic which was the only place in Cairo with an x-ray machine at the time. The discovery of the ice-man in the Tyrol practically induced mass hysteria in anthropologists and they volunteered in droves to get their hands on him, or a piece of him.[1] The world was also treated to the unedifying sight of Austria and Italy squabbling over his ownership and Ötzi was put into cold storage pending the resolution of this vital diplomatic issue.

Mummies, bog bodies and ice-men can confidently expect extensive media coverage and, in the fullness of time, many scholarly works and richly illustrated books to be written about them. But, although these kinds of human remains may have considerable value for those who examine them, there is relatively little to be gained from their study, since single cases generally do not provide any information which can be referred to the population from which that individual or individuals came. Anthropologists or bone specialists, however, cannot resist them, and in this respect they are rather like doctors who cannot resist a rare case. Sitting in an outpatient clinic all morning, seeing a run of patients with common ailments is compensated for by the fact that the next person through the door may have a deliciously rare complaint which may be the subject of a paper in the medical press or at least a presentation at the next grand round.

For years, skeletons were largely ignored as a source of information about the past, which is surprising when one considers that the business of archaeologists and historians is to reconstruct past societies, and the most proximate of all the relics of the past were frequently discarded by archaeologists in their anxiety to recover other artefacts. When archaeologists or bone specialists (BS from now on) did choose to study the skeleton, they often restricted their attention to the skull, discarding the rest of the skeleton, the post-cranial bones being seen as of no value. To the skull they devoted much time and effort in taking an enormous series of measurements which they hoped would provide them with information on race and migration, for example. This practice was especially common during the first 30 or 40 years of the last century, and was described by Saul Jarcho as 'cranial fixation'.[2]

Medical men in particular had long been interested in disease in antiquity, and the study of palaeopathology dates back to the early part of the nineteenth century. The first great impetus to the study of disease in human remains was provided by the discovery of huge amounts of Native American remains during the push to the west. As the settlers and the army moved through the interior of America, they discovered great mounds of bones which, naturally, they desecrated. The skulls attracted the greatest interest and were dispersed and examined. The army doctors were among the foremost to examine these remains and the first systematic study of disease in human remains was made by Joseph Jones who published his findings in a monograph in 1876.[3] Jones purported to find evidence of syphilis among the remains which he examined, and there was subsequently considerable interest in this disease among the earliest of the palaeopathologists, an interest which has recently been awakened and which will be considered later.

There was nothing in the Old World to rival the Indian mounds until the Egyptian government decided to raise the Aswan Dam in 1907. The dam had been built in 1902 to improve the irrigation of the cotton crop in Lower and Middle Egypt, but when it was completed many archaeological sites were lost, and the famous temple at Philae had been inundated. Raising the dam would inevitably result in the loss of further archaeological sites and so it was decided to excavate as much as possible in advance.

The excavation was under the direction of the American archaeologist George Reisner, and it was hoped that the study of the human remains would not only enable the culture of the people who had once inhabited the area to be reconstructed, but also their race and ethnological affinities. The man chosen to examine the human remains was Elliot Smith who, with Frederic Wood Jones and Douglas Derry studied upwards of 6,000 bodies in very short time.

Smith and Wood Jones published the account of their findings in a series of bulletins in a monograph which appeared in 1910. The report[4] is rather disappointing in that it is difficult to find exactly what the structure of the populations were that they studied, their description of the pathology is somewhat inadequate, and it has not been possible to determine what the prevalence was of any of the diseases which they found. A few papers were published in the medical press dealing with some of the diseases which were found, but neither Smith nor Wood Jones took much further interest in palaeopathology after they left Egypt — Elliot Smith to become professor of anatomy in Manchester, and Frederic Wood Jones to travel the world, occupying several chairs of anatomy — the importance of their work in Nubia was substantially diminished.[5]

Those who first studied human remains tended to be anatomists rather than pathologists, and in the first half of the last century anatomists were much more interested in fossil remains than those of more recent origin. Fossils attracted the same degree of public attention that bog bodies do nowadays but the anatomists were woefully led astray by the discovery of the fossils at Piltdown. Much time was spent trying to fit him into the mainstream of evolution and bitter feuds were conducted by some of the more famous anatomists of the day, who entered into vehement disagreements about the precise construction of the skull and other matters. Sad to think that friendships were lost over what turned out to be nothing more than a fraud.

Revival of interest in human remains of the more mundane nature did not start again until after the Second World War, and in this country at least is associated in large part with the name of Calvin Wells. Calvin was a general practitioner in Norfolk having started out before the war to become an obstetrician. Quite why he did not go back to obstetrics after the war is unclear, but he settled in Norfolk and began to work with the archaeologists in Norwich and elsewhere. His particular interest was in palaeopathology and he was extremely encouraging to newcomers to the field, so long as they were medically qualified. He was very firmly of the view that a medical qualification was an absolute requirement for taking up palaeopathology, and he could be vituperative about those who worked in the area but were not fortunate to have the advantage he enjoyed himself. For many years after the war he was virtually the only person in the country whose publications on palaeopathology were cited in the *Index Medicus*. He writing was clear and mercifully almost free of jargon, and his book *Bones, Bodies and Disease*[6] introduced a great many people to palaeopathology and I am included amongst that number. The narrative moves along at great pace and the book is still a good read, an exemplar of the interpretive school of palaeopathology which still has many adherents.

Calvin was almost certainly the worst driver in the world, and being driven from his cottage to the department of archaeology in the Castle Museum in Norwich was one of the most fearful experiences of my life as he talked incessantly, mostly with his face turned in his passenger's direction. He was aware that he was virtually alone in keeping palaeopathology alive in Britain and he shrewdly realised that archaeologists no less than the general public liked a good story; this led him to over-interpret the changes he found in the skeletons he examined. He would confidently predict the occupation of a skeleton on the basis of curvature of the spine, or from a particular pattern of osteoarthritis, even though the evidence was tenuous to say the least. On the last occasion I saw him he took me to see a skeleton from a Romano-British site which had periostitis around both ankles. He asked me what I thought the explanation was, immediately giving his own interpretation that it was the reaction to being shackled at the ankle, and that the individual must have been a slave. The more mundane explanation that it was probably the result of venous stasis and that the poor man had had varicose veins did not appeal to him at all.

Wells's insistence that palaeopathology was a discipline into which only those with a medical qualification could be admitted raises the issue of its role within larger areas of study. There is almost no one nowadays who would support Calvin's point of view — or at least admit to it — and by far the majority of BS have been trained in physical anthropology or archaeology and have no specialist medical or pathological knowledge. This ensures that many elementary clinical errors are made by those without medical training who too easily assume that there must be an answer to *everything*. Those who have gone through the medical mill know — although they may not acknowledge — that many of the patients they see will never get a definitive diagnosis, or that the diagnosis they *are* given stands a very high chance of being wrong. There have been several studies which have shown that clinicians are poor diagnosticians, and that they may misdiagnose their patients in up to a third of cases. There are many reasons for this, and this is not the place to go into this matter further, except to say that if clinicians get it wrong when they have the advantage of talking to their patients and taking a history — who can order virtually any number of laboratory, radiological and other investigations — then there is precious little hope for BS to get it all *right* with the limited means at their disposal. It is quite common at meetings of BS for specimens to be brought and touted round for a diagnosis; when shown to the medical doctors present, the response is very likely to be a shake of the head from the doctor and a tut of impatience from the BS asking the question. Later the same doctor will be told by the same BS that the lesion in question *is* undoubtedly rheumatoid arthritis (or whatever), since X (or Y) has pronounced it to be so. After a while, the irritation felt by this wanes, and — fortunately — repeated protestations of ignorance mean that one is not asked any more.

So, while it is not *necessary* to have a medical training in order to become a BS it generally does no harm if palaeopathology is to included within the BS's remit. If it is not, then a training in physical anthropology will better equip the BS for studying human remains than a medical course. This is not to say that palaeopathology is a medical discipline, rather, in my view, it is part of medical history. The objective of studying human remains must be to develop an understanding of the nature of past populations and this is an aim shared with historians and archaeologists. Historians and archaeologists use data of particular kinds in their work, and so do BS; in their case, the physical remains of the populations they are trying to reconstruct. Naturally, each discipline wishes to extract the maximum amount of information from the data they study, and this book examines what may reasonably be expected from the study of human remains. If I seem to concentrate too much on the limitations of such work, it is because there has been — and still is — rather too much emphasis on what one might call the optimistic interpretations.

Part 1: Life

1 Ageing and sexing

Ageing and sexing — once described to me by an eminent BS as a way of life — is the most fundamental aspect of studying human remains, and although one feels intuitively that it should be straightforward, it is actually full of pitfalls and many a BS has made a career of introducing new methods for doing it. Looking round at any group of living people makes it abundantly clear that there are significant differences in physique between males and females and between individuals of varying age. These changes are reflected in the morphology of the skeleton and form the basis of estimating both age and sex.

Ageing

Ageing the skeleton depends in the main upon two factors: the development and eruption of the teeth, and the growth and development of the long bones of the arms and legs. Dental development in infants follows a regular pattern in which the tooth buds develop, the roots are formed, the apices fuse, and the teeth erupt through the gums to become visible in the mouth. Humans have two sets of teeth and the pattern of development of both proceeds in an orderly manner. Many studies have been carried out in living populations to determine the age at which the various teeth, both deciduous and permanent, erupt. The stages of tooth formation have also been studied in great detail, especially with the help of x-rays. Many charts are available which show the average age at which the different teeth form and erupt and these are widely used by BS to age sub-adult skeletons.[1] The wisdom teeth are the last to erupt which they usually do by about the age of 20 if they are going to do so at all. In a substantial proportion of the population they never do erupt.

It seems to be generally agreed that dental development is reasonably constant and provides a reliable indication of age — in modern populations at least. This brings us up against an important consideration in bone studies; that is, can we be sure that the rate of dental development was the same in past populations as it is now? How safe are we in applying present day standards to the past? The answer, of course, is that we do not know for certain, but there is no theoretical reason why they should not be the same. Dental development is under genetic control and although it can be affected by environmental factors such as malnutrition or disease, there is no likelihood that there will have been a big change in the genetic component in the relatively short time involved with most bone studies. In this country, for example, no populations of bones older that the Neolithic are studied and there can have been no significant change in the gene pool between then and now.

Where the teeth survive then, ageing of infants and juveniles is straightforward and (one supposes) reasonably accurate; that is to say, the age derived from the skeleton is likely to closely approximate the real age of the child at death. In other words, one can derive the *chronological* age of the child. Unfortunately, children's skulls and mandibles are rather fragile and easily damaged; the teeth — especially the tooth buds — are also small and may be overlooked during excavation. When there are no teeth, other methods have to be used to age sub-adult skeletons.

A reasonable estimate of the chronological age of a sub-adult can be determined from the stage of development of the long bones. During infancy and childhood the long bones consist of three parts, a central shaft (or diaphysis) and two ends (or epiphyses). Each epiphysis is connected to the diaphysis by a region of cartilage known as the metaphysis; it is by laying down bone at the metaphysis that the long bones grow in length. At some point, usually starting just before puberty, the ends of the bones fuse permanently to the shaft and they assume their final length. Epiphyseal fusion takes place in an orderly sequence and, as with dental eruption, the ages at which the various bones in the body fuse is well known.[2] The age range at which fusion takes place is wider than for dental eruption and so any estimate of age which is based on this phenomenon is likely to be less accurate. Nevertheless, in a well preserved juvenile skeleton, a satisfactory estimate of age should be obtained from the pattern of fusion, and this would certainly be expected with a modern child and the method is important in forensic science.

Although bodies are frequently incomplete when they are recovered there will often be sufficient of the long bones present in a juvenile to allow an estimate of age to be made from the pattern of epiphyseal closure. For example, with an incomplete male skeleton in which the upper end of the humerus was unfused, the lower end fused, the distal end of the tibia fusing and the proximal end of the clavicle unfused, it would be reasonable to place the age at between 19 and 30, and most probably closer to 19 than 30.

In juveniles who are not approaching puberty and in whom the epiphyses are not fusing, then — if there are no teeth — some help can be obtained from the length of the long bone shafts. The length of the arms and legs is obviously related to age and there are some modern tables of bone lengths in boys and girls of different ages obtained from radiographic studies;[3] studies which can never be repeated because of the hazards of radiation. These modern studies are not directly applicable to children who lived in the past as we know that bone growth in childhood was slower in the past than it is now, and using modern standard tables would tend to underestimate the ages of the children.[4] The most satisfactory way to use bone lengths in children to assess their age is by using internal data. The lengths of the long bones are always routinely measured in any examination of human bones and it is then easy to construct a table in which the lengths of the major long bones are related to the age as determined from dental eruption. The long bone lengths of those skeletons in which the teeth have not survived can simply be fitted into the table and by this method, the age can be determined.

With foetal skeletons there is virtually no other way to derive an age other than from long bone measurements. Tables of measurements at various stages of foetal development have been published, usually by forensic scientists.[5] Foetal or neonatal bones are not uncommon in cemetery excavations, and estimates of gestational age have to rely on measurements. Whether modern data can validly be used for this purpose is arguable, but as there are no other data available, this is the best that can be done in this situation. In fact, the modern data probably *are* reliable; foetal development is very constant in terms of time and the great majority of babies are born at or around nine months after conception. And while there is no doubt that maternal nutrition may well have been poorer in the past than it is now, the foetus is a very successful parasite, nourished in preference to the mother when supplies are scarce, so it is likely that foetal weights throughout gestation will not have altered markedly over time.

Ageing sub-adult skeletons is — by the standards of bone work — relatively easy and, at least when carried out using tooth eruption, a reliable chronological age can be arrived at. Once the epiphyses have fused, however, things change markedly for the worse, and for adults many BS will talk about determining biological, as opposed to chronological age. This is because the ageing of adult skeletons depends upon the changes which take place in the morphology of the skeleton with advancing age and there is no *a priori* reason why these changes should proceed at the same pace in all individuals.

Many methods have been described for ageing adult skeletons, and there are gangs of postgraduate students in departments of physical anthropology sweating over devising new ones for their dissertations. The fact that so many methods have been described indicates that none is entirely satisfactory. It may not be of the greatest importance that the age of an adult skeleton from an archaeological assemblage is accurately determined but it certainly is when dealing with forensic material. Where is *does* matter for BS is when they attempt to study the pattern of disease with increasing age; they will not be able to do this if they cannot have some confidence in their ageing techniques.

Probably most BS rely on dental wear as a measure of determining age. This is a method which can be used for populations which had a tough diet but is not much use for skeletons from eighteenth- or nineteenth-century cemeteries since they will have had a much softer diet and their teeth will show relatively little wear. Fortunately for the BS, a number of individuals have devoted many of their working years to producing charts of tooth wear which can be applied by their colleagues.[6] This method works best when there is a full set of teeth for examination, but all too frequently teeth are missing or so decayed or damaged that the wear pattern cannot be determined with any confidence. The BS then has to turn to other methods, the most important being the morphology of the pubic symphysis and the distal end of the fourth rib; some BS may also use the state of fusion of the cranial sutures, but this is regarded nowadays as being so inconsistent that the majority of BS do not use it any more.

The pubic symphysis joins the two pubic bones in the front of the pelvis by fibro-cartilage. The bone to which the fibro-cartilage is joined starts out being very rugose with a variable number of ridges which are easily seen in the skeleton. With increasing age, the ridges flatten and new bone is formed around the margins of the joint. This process has been studied in skeletons from collections of modern skeletons of known age and the changes have been grouped into a number of stages, corresponding to age categories in both males and female.[7] Casts are available of the type specimens from each category and these are to be found among the debris on most BS's work tables. Again, they generally give thanks to the selfless individuals who have carried out the work necessary to produce the casts and shell out the money to buy them without demur.

The end of the first seven ribs are joined to the sternum by cartilage; the underlying distal end of the rib is smooth during the early years of life but gradual ossification takes place into the costal cartilage and new bone develops around the circumference of the rib end. Again, these changes — in the first and fourth ribs — have been studied in modern collections and the stages have been published and can be used to age adult skeletons.[8]

Unfortunately, it is not unusual for the pubic symphysis to be damaged, either by the processes which happen after burial or during excavation, and the same is true of the ribs. No teeth, no pubic symphysis and no ribs — no age. Wherever possible, BS will try not to rely on a single ageing criterion, but will use information from teeth, pubis and ribs to derive an ageing 'score' which they can hopefully translate into an age range. It is never possible to age an adult skeleton very closely and any publication which presents the ages of adults to within a year or two should be viewed at best with considerable scepticism — and preferably discounted altogether. The best any competent BS can do is to present ages with a five year range, and my own preference is to present them in ten year ranges, 25-34, 35-44 and so on.

Some BS make what I consider to be the major error of ageing skeletons on the basis of pathological changes, particularly the presence of new bone around joint margins — so-called marginal osteophytes, or of osteoarthritis. Now while it is certainly true that both become increasingly common with age, using them as ageing criteria destroys any possibility of studying the frequency with which they occur in an assemblage at different ages and much potentially interesting information is thereby lost.

The unreliability of methods to age the adult skeleton is the spur to trying to find other more reliable tests and there have been a few studies in which ageing techniques have been applied to skeletons of known age at death to see which is most reliable. One such study was carried out on a group of skeletons recovered from the crypt of Christ Church, Spitalfields. The conditions within the crypt were such that a considerable number of coffin plates had survived giving the name, age, date of death and sometimes the occupation of the incumbent. These skeletons were aged (and sexed) by a single observer who found that the younger skeletons tended to be over-aged and the older skeletons under-aged.[9] Great weight was given to the fact that one individual carried out all the observations, but, unfortunately, this tended to diminish rather than enhance the validity of the findings, since it could be argued that it was not the methods but the observer which was in error. A much better study design would have been to have at least two, and preferably three, observers examining all the skeletons after a period of training in which they could demonstrate that there were no serious inter-observer errors in the use of the methods. Sites where skeletons of known age at death are not common, but it is to be hoped that when the next opportunity arises, advice will be sought from an epidemiologist before the study is in hand.

Perhaps I could leave this section on ageing with a reference to David Birkett who was a delightful man with an infectious iconoclasm. He died tragically in 1990 and was a tremendous loss to palaeopathology. David was not slow in his criticism of sloppy thinking, and during one tedious discussion on the subject of ageing skeletons he said, supposedly *sotto voce* but loud enough for most people in the audience to hear, 'Why don't we just say that they're all post-natal? At least no one can argue with that!'

Sexing

From what has gone before, it will be evident that it is easier to age a sub-adult skeleton than an adult. When it comes to sexing, however, the converse is the case; adult skeletons can be sexed with relative ease, whereas juvenile skeletons cannot be sexed reliably using conventional methods.

The methods of sexing adults is based on the changes which take place at puberty when the female pelvis is adapted to house and then deliver a baby. The shapes of the adult male and female pelvises are very distinct and in the majority of cases, very easy to distinguish. (As with all things biological, this is rather an overstatement and females with male-like pelvises and vice versa occur all too frequently for the comfort of most BS.) The male pelvis has been described as a long segment of a narrow cone, and the female as a short segment of a broad cone. In the male the sciatic notch has a much more acute angle than the female as does the pubic arch.[10] The female pubic arch has to accommodate the foetal head during delivery and so it has to be much broader than in the male. These are the major changes; there are others, for example, the height of the pubic symphysis is less in the female than in the male and the auricular surface of the sacro-iliac joint has a different configuration. Where the pelvis is well preserved there should be little difficulty in accurately determining the sex of a skeleton. The pelvis may not survive all that well, however; the pubis in particular is prone to damage as it tends to be crushed under the weight of soil after burial. When this is the case, the BS turns to the skull.

If you look around you the next time you are in a crowd it will not take you long to see the differences in the anatomy of the male and female skull. The male is more robust, usually has a larger, often square jaw, and has well-developed brow ridges. These features are more apparent in the defleshed skull; in addition there are some other features which will help distinguish the sexes. The mastoid process is more robust and longer than in males in females, and the area of the occiput into which the muscles of the neck are attached is more roughened. There are some other minor features which may be used if the more important diagnostic elements are damaged or missing, but with an intact skull, there should not be much difficulty in accurately assigning a sex. The usual caveat applies, of course: there are females with male-like skulls and males with female-like skulls, but nobody said it was *that* easy.

Not infrequently both pelvis and skull are missing or too poorly preserved to offer much help to the BS who must then take recourse to other, less reliable methods. The next best way to proceed is to use some measurements and those most commonly used are the maximum diameters of the femoral and humeral heads, the maximum length of the clavicle and the glenoid of the scapula. In males and females each of these measurements falls with a certain range but there is an overlap between the highest values in females and the lowest value in male so that it is not possible to separate them absolutely. In British skeletons from virtually all periods, it is found that where the head of the humerus or the femur is equal or greater than 45mm, then the skeleton is likely to be male. Similarly, where the maximum length of the glenoid is equal or greater than 35mm, or the maximum length of the clavicle equal to or greater than 145mm, the skeleton is probably male. The further away these values are from the so-called cutting point, then the more confidence one can have of the maleness or femaleness of the skeleton; and it is always better to rely on several measurements than on one.

The values which have been derived from British populations to discriminate between the sexes may well not be applicable to skeletons from elsewhere. Quite a number of BS work in Egypt (when they can get the chance) and the skeletons recovered there are much smaller than those from British sites and they cannot be sexed using British norms. In this case, and in cases where there is doubt about the validity of using the standard discriminant functions, two methods can be applied. Firstly, the measurements from skeletons where the sex can confidently be determined from the pelvis or skull can be tabulated (as with the bone lengths in children) and measurements from otherwise unsexed skeletons compared with these. Secondly, all the values from the assemblage can be plotted and the point of overlap noted from the graph; this value can be used as the sectioning point, recognising that there will be increasing certainty in the assignment of sex the further the measurements diverge from this point.

What to do about the pair of legs or the jumble of battered bones in a bag with no pelvis, skull or complete bone ends? The temptation will be quickly to return the bits to the bag and pass on to the next box with a complete skeleton, especially if it is late in the day and the sounds of wine being uncorked can be heard. All is not entirely lost, however, as it may be possible to make a best guess from the size and shape of what bones there are. Large, heavy robust limb bones with well-developed muscle markings are not likely to be from a female — not in the past, anyway. Conversely, short, gracile bones will seldom be from a male. This is certainly not an assessment on which one would like to place great weight and you would not bet your mortgage on it, but with experience it is possible to assign a probable sex to what sometimes seems the most unpromising material. Having said that, however, in any assemblage there will remain a proportion — sometimes a significant proportion — of skeletons to which one cannot assign a sex and the question of how to deal with them will be considered in chapter 8.

That one cannot distinguish between the skeletons of pre-pubertal males and females is a bit of a surprise. There is no difficulty doing so during life and the most casual observer will readily notice that the physique of boys and girls is different, even at relatively young ages. The differences do not seem to be reflected in the skeleton, however, and although attempts have been made to find distinguishing features, none has been entirely successful. It has been suggested that the shape and depth of the sciatic notch can discriminate between foetal skeletons, and some very preliminary work which my colleagues and I have undertaken is promising, but no more than that. The maximum length of the canine has sometimes been mooted, but even if this were to prove an acceptable discriminator, it can only be used in older children when the tooth has been finally formed.

Recently, a method of sexing skeletons has been described which relies on the ability to extract DNA from the skeleton.[11] Until a few years ago the orthodox view was that bones recovered from archaeological sites consisted entirely of inorganic material and that all the organic material — collagen and bone and serum proteins, for example — had long decayed. It was a considerable surprise, then, when it proved possible to extract DNA from bones — what is now referred to as ancient DNA, or aDNA. In the first instance attempts were made only to extract mitochondrial DNA as it was felt that this was the most likely to survive in bone, but it was soon found that genomic DNA was also preserved — albeit in a much damaged state — and this led the way for the development of methods to sex ancient skeletons. The method relies upon a technique known as the polymerase chain reaction (PCR) which is able to amplify degraded copies of aDNA so that the material comes to be present in sufficient quantity to be detectable. For sexing the skeleton, PCR is used to amplify that part of the aDNA that contains the gene for the production of amelogenin, the tooth enamel protein. The gene is found on both the X and the Y chromosomes but is smaller (contains fewer bases) on the Y chromosome. The region on the aDNA is amplified and then separated by electrophoresis, when males will be found to have two copies of the gene but females only one. This method has been used by several groups to determine the sex of skeletons, and my colleagues and I used it to validate the use of the morphology of the sciatic notch as a means of sexing foetuses. We had only a small sample to begin with, and we could not extract aDNA from them all; nevertheless, the method looked sufficiently promising to try it out with larger numbers of skeletons.[12]

PCR is available only at specialised centres and it is never likely to become widely available to the BS and should not be undertaken by those without the necessary training and expertise. It is also quite expensive and this alone would mitigate against it being used as a routine in archaeology. For forensic work, where cost implications are not quite so over-riding, it is an invaluable method, especially as DNA will be much better preserved in more recent bone. For bone studies its main use will be to answer particular research questions. Our study was carried out on babies from a Romano-British site and we hoped that we might be able to develop a reliable morphological method for sexing in order to throw some light on the suggestion that infanticide of female children was preferentially carried out during that period. If there is an approximately equal number of neonatal skeletons of both sexes from the Romano-British period, then this hypothesis seems unlikely. On the other hand, if a substantial surplus of girl babies were to be found, then it becomes much more plausible. PCR could also be used — in skeletons of all ages — if it were important to know the sex of an individual skeleton. Were the skeletons found in the Tower of London really those of the princes supposedly killed by Richard II? If it could be shown that they were actually female, this would be certainly show that they were *not*; on the other hand, if they *were* male, the case would not be greatly advanced. PCR has also assumed some importance in confirming the diagnosis of some infectious diseases, as will be discussed later.

2 Height and weight

One of the most widely held beliefs about people in the past, certainly among the lay public, is that they were much shorter than we are, but skeletal evidence does not entirely support this view. The height of the skeleton can be calculated from the maximum length of the limb bones thanks mostly to the work of Mildred Trotter and her colleague Goldine Gleser. Using data obtained from the bodies of American soldiers killed in the Second World War and in the Korean War, and the bodies of civilians from the Terry Collection now in the Smithsonian Institution, they developed a series of equations which could be used for the determination of height from the skeleton.[1] The heights of the soldiers were known from their army records, and those of the subjects from the Terry Collection were measured directly from the cadaver. The length of each of the long bones was taken after any necessary cleaning, and from all the information that had been collected Trotter and Gleser produced a series of equations of which the following is typical:

$$\text{Height} = 2.38 \text{ x Maximum femoral length (cm)} = 61.41 \pm 3.27$$

Trotter and Gleser produced an equation to use with each of the six limb bones of the arms and legs and each is associated with a standard error term (the ± value shown at the end of the equation). It is good practice to use the measurement which has the lowest error term as this will introduce the least error into the calculation. The 'true' height of the individual will then be contained with the range derived by adding or subtracting the error term to the answer obtained when the maximum height of the bone is substituted in the equation. For example, if the height obtained from a measurement of the femur is 170cm ± 0.3cm, then the 'true' height will lie somewhere between 167-173cm.

This is all very well, but we can see again the problem which has cropped up in other connections; that is, how reliable are modern American data for calculating heights in individuals long dead? The answer revolves around the extent to which one might consider that limb proportions may have changed over the centuries, and, in my view, it not likely to have been very much. It may be argued that modern Americans are likely to be taller than ancient Britons, but if they are, then the reason is to be found in better nutrition rather than in any other factor. And while poor nutrition may result in a failure to achieve the potential maximum height, it seems barely credible that it would affect arm or leg length disproportionately and the application of Trotter's equations does seem reasonable.

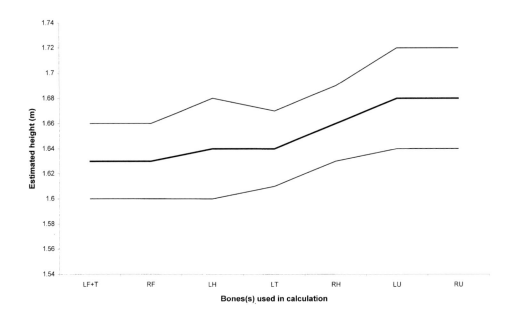

1   *Estimate of height obtained from different long bone measurements with upper and lower limits obtained from height ± standard error. LF+T = left femur + tibia; RF = right femur; LH = left humerus; LT = left tibia; RH = right humerus; LU = left ulna; RU = right ulna*

Even if it were *not* reasonable to apply them it would not matter so long as the resultant heights were used to make comparisons between the heights of different ancient populations. Many BS use Trotter's equations and the results which are obtained from their use can be said to be standardised. That is to say, since everyone uses the same method of calculating height from the skeleton, the results are directly comparable from one study to another even though the height may not be the actual height of the individual during life. If the purpose of calculating height is to track changes across time, then whether or not one is dealing with the real height or a standardised height is immaterial. For comparisons with the height of modern individuals, however, the difference is important, but, as I have already said, it is probable that Trotter's equation will give a good estimate of the real height, so long as certain caveats are taken into account.

A more serious criticism of the way in which Trotter's equations are used — and this is a criticism of BS and not of Trotter — is that when calculating heights, use is made of *any* intact limb bone, excepting that, where there is a choice, the one which is associated with the smallest error term is used. Thus, when the heights of the skeletal assemblage at large are presented, the table or graph will be a mixture of heights calculated from the femur, the tibia, the radius, the humerus and so on. When a skeleton presents itself with all the limb bones intact and where the height can be calculated using each of Trotter's equations, the results are very salutary. In figure **1**, the results are shown for a complete

Table 1 Estimation of mean heights (m) for a medieval skeletal assemblage based on measurements of any bone, or of femur only. SD = standard deviation

		Number	Mean	SD	Range
Male	Any bone	79	1.66	0.09	1.47-1.81
	Femur only	57	1.70	0.06	1.58-1.81
Female	Any bone	60	1.59	0.05	1.49-1.78
	Femur only	45	1.58	0.06	1.49-1.77

medieval skeleton and it can be seen that the heights obtained vary considerably, by as much as 5cm. If the standard errors are taken into account, it can be seen that the 'true' height of this skeleton may vary by as much as 12cm; 1.6-1.72m from least to greatest. The use of any bone, willy nilly, will introduce so much error into the calculation of the mean height of an assemblage that it is scarcely worth putting the results into print — but of course they will be and no mention is likely to be made of any difficulties which might arise therefrom!

What remedies are available then to overcome this problem? There are two — at least. The first is to use only one bone when calculating height and the bone of choice is the femur. The femur is a robust bone and generally survives burial well so that in any skeletal assemblage a substantial proportion of the skeletons will have intact femurs. If they have been broken post mortem they can often be mended prior to measuring; I have heard some BS deride this practice as being so liable to introduce error into the calculation, that it must on no account be undertaken. Compared with the other errors involved, the tiny error introduced by mending a broken bone with a bit of masking tape is too trivial to bother with.

When only the femur is used to calculate the heights of a skeletal assemblage and the results compared with those obtained when any bone is used, some interesting results are obtained. In **Table 1**, I have shown the results for two medieval assemblages.[2] When the heights of male skeletons are calculated using only the femur, the mean height is significantly reduced (significant in the statistical rather that the biological sense); using only the femur *reduces* the mean height of the males in both cases by approximately 4-5cm. By contrast, the mean height of the females is scarcely, if at all, affected. The reason for this is that the upper and lower limbs of females are more equally proportioned than in males. These results strongly suggest that there is good reason to use *only* the femur when calculating heights even though this will inevitably result in fewer — though more reliable — data. Furthermore, if one is interested only in comparing heights between different ancient populations, then there is no reason why the maximum height of the femur should not be used without further manipulation. After all, in this instance, the *actual* height is not a matter for consideration, only changes which have occurred over time, and for this, femoral height is perfectly adequate. Old habits die hard, however, and there is

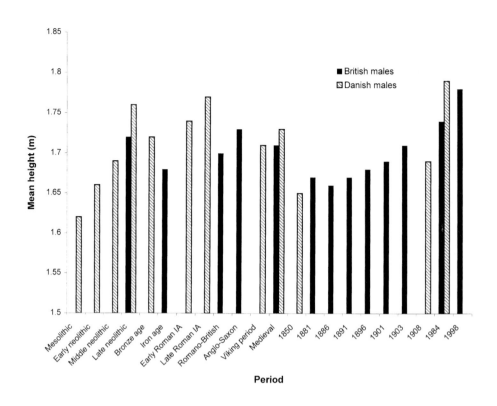

2 *Mean heights for different British and Danish male skeletons. Note that the time scale is not shown in equal increments*

not much prospect that BS will be able to resist calculating height using whatever bone is to hand; in passing perhaps I should note that there are even equations which purport to allow height to be determined from segments of broken bone. How accurate the results obtained from these equations are likely to be I leave to the imagination of the reader.

To return to the statement of belief mentioned at the start of this chapter, is there any evidence to support the view that our ancestors were shorter — perhaps much shorter — than we are? The best evidence that we have indicates that there were differences, but that at most periods they were not very great until very recently. In figure **2** I have shown the results from studies which I have conducted on male skeletons from different sites in Britain, and also the results of studies on Danish male skeletons, published by Pia Bennike.[3] It will be seen that the mean height of British males was at all times less than it is today, the maximum difference being shown by the Iron Age population which was, on average, 6mm shorter than the 1984 mean. There is no consistent trend in the data up to the medieval period and the range in all periods is considerable and all overlap the modern data. In the last decade or so, there seems to have been a considerable increase in mean male height[4] which exaggerates the differences in height between modern and past populations.

28

The Danish data show a considerable increase in height from Mesolithic to late Neolithic, but thereafter the means fluctuate considerably. The heights of the very early Danish populations are considerably less than in later populations and probably represent real biological differences although the numbers in these early samples are small and never greater than 10.

The Danish data show that during the middle of the nineteenth century and the beginning of the twentieth males were, on average, shorter than at any time since the early Neolithic. A similar substantial reduction in height occurred in Britain during the nineteenth century. In 1904 an Inter-Departmental Committee presented a Report to Parliament detailing its findings in relation to an enquiry into the supposed physical deterioration of the population.[5] The enquiry had been instigated because so many volunteers for army service during the Crimean and Boer wars had failed to meet the not very stringent physical standards required. The Committee showed that the average height of young men applying to join the Post Office in 1881 had been 1.67m — less than the height of men in the Neolithic. It rose steadily up until 1903 when the average reached 1.71m, equal to the mean height during the medieval period. There seems to be little doubt that the short stature noted during the nineteenth century was connected with industrialisation and urbanisation, the most important factor being an impoverished diet, as was suggested by the Committee. Improvements in nutrition during the twentieth century have permitted British males to achieve the mean height of our Neolithic and Anglo-Saxon forebears, surpassing them substantially only as the century ended.[6]

The importance of being able to determine and compare heights (or surrogates of height such as maximum femoral length) is that final achieved height is probably the best index of nutritional status. As such, it is a matter of some interest to historians as well as to BS and archaeologists. The historians, of course, rely on documentary evidence which has often been obtained from royal or upper class families. Some historians *are* inclined to the view that earlier populations were much shorter and I remember an occasion on which I was at a meeting of historians and BS to discuss this point. One of the historians present put forward that view and when I ventured to say that the skeletal evidence did not bear this out, I was told that 'in that case, the skeletons are wrong'!

It is probably true that juveniles and sub-adults were shorter for their age than at present. The site of Barton-on-Humber has yielded approximately 3,000 skeletons from a cemetery that was used from the Anglo-Saxon period up to the early nineteenth century. There are many hundreds of sub-adult skeletons in the assemblage and when we looked at the maximum length of the long bones at age intervals determined by tooth eruption, it was found that all the individuals were shorter than would be expected today.[7] By contrast, the height of the adults shows little variation over the years and the mean is similar to the 1984 mean.[8] The most reasonable interpretation of these data is that growth continued for a longer period in the past and that final height was achieved some years later than at present, as Tanner suggested some years ago.[9]

Prediction of physique

It would be interesting if, in addition to calculating height, we were also able to predict physique and weight from the skeleton. Bones respond to stresses imposed upon them by increasing in size, and strenuous muscular activity may result in the muscle insertions becoming enlarged. One only has to look at the difference in size of the arms of professional tennis players to see the truth of this. It seems probable, then, that a robust skeleton would denote an individual with a robust physique; conversely, it is not likely that an individual with a gracile skeleton would have a robust physique. Two indices are used to represent physique, the body mass index (BMI) and the ponderal index (PI). The BMI is derived from the formula

$$BMI = weight/height^2$$

and the PI is derived as

$$PI = height/weight^{0.33}$$

Regression equations have been derived from measurements in a large sample of modern subjects by which BMI and PI can be calculated within reasonable limits and for determining the physique of fossil hominids.[10] The best skeletal predictors of BMI and PI vary according to which author's work one consults, but measures of tibial length and width, the maximum diameter of the femoral or humeral head, and the diameters of the superior surface of the lumbar vertebrae have all been found to yield good estimates.

I am not aware that any large scale estimates of body size have been made on recent adult populations, but it would be of interest to look at how body size has altered over the centuries and relate it to changes in the pattern and frequency of some diseases; osteoarthritis in particular. Generally those who study body size concentrate on fossils and each new fossil may end up getting the treatment. Porter, for example, has reported on the results obtained when he applied his equations to the tibial fragment of Boxgrove man.[11] The fragment was found at the Palaeolithic site of Boxgrove in southern England and was described by those who first examined it as being 'massive'. Certainly the photograph which accompanied the original description of the bone in *Nature* showed a very thickened cortex[12] but when Porter examined a cast of the bone he found that the bone was not unduly robust when compared with modern tibias. My own first impression was the thickened cortex was pathological and that perhaps Boxgrove man had suffered from some condition such as Paget's disease. Porter concluded that Boxgrove man was indeed male and estimated his height to be 1.80m with a BMI of 21.9 and a PI of 43.3; Porter's suggested that this individual was built for strength rather than speed.

A study of some children who had been buried in a cemetery attached to an orphans' home in Sydney in the nineteenth century showed — perhaps unsurprisingly — that they were shorter and lighter for their age than comparable nineteenth-century children.[13] The sample size was small, but the equations which were derived to estimate weight seemed robust when applied to children of known weight and, again, it would be interesting to repeat the estimates with other groups of children, especially as the health of children has been rather neglected to date.

3 The working life

We have seen in the previous chapter that it is possible to predict physique from the skeleton at least to some degree; at least we can say that robust bones mean a robust physique, gracile bones indicate a slight physique. Is it possible to go further? Can we predict what kind of work was undertaken by individuals on the basis of the morphology of, or the pathology found in, their bones? Most BS would like to be able to do so, and some actually believe that they can do so; this optimism is admirable but — as I hope to show in this chapter — misplaced.

When BS attribute an occupation to a skeleton they usually do on the basis of pathological changes, most usually on the basis of the pattern of osteoarthritis found in the skeleton. We will discuss osteoarthritis (OA) in more detail in a later chapter; suffice it to say at present that it is a joint disease which is common and pretty easy to diagnose in the skeleton. There have been many modern epidemiological studies of the prevalence of OA among working populations and some associations have been found as shown in **Table 2**. The most convincing studies to date have been those which have shown that farmers are much more at risk of developing OA of the hip than the general population; they have something like a nine-fold risk of developing this disease.[1] The association between farming and OA of the hip has been found in several countries but the cause is not known; it seems to apply equally to arable and dairy farmers and no convincing explanation has yet appeared.

At this point it is necessary to introduce some cautionary words before anyone starts to get too excited. Firstly, there are studies which have failed to show an association between occupation and the development of OA, although these do not generally get the attention that is accorded to the positive studies. Secondly, many of those who undertake heavy manual work do not get OA and, conversely, many of those engaged in sedentary work do. Heavy work, therefore, is not a necessary condition for the development of OA.

Thirdly, none of the associations which have been found between occupation and OA is what might be called site-specific. That is to say, it is not only farmers who get OA of the hip, or miners who get OA of the spine, and the number of non-farmers with OA of the hip will be much greater than the number of farmers with it.

Finally, there are several factors other than occupation which might lead to the development of OA. These include activity, a genetic predisposition, age, sex, weight, trauma, race in addition to possible contributions from occupation (**3**). The most important factor is activity; joint movement is a *sine qua non* for the development of OA;

Table 2 Relationship between some occupations and the site of development of osteoarthritis (OA). Note that in ballet dancers and footballers OA is usually consequent upon trauma. In mill workers the tasks carried out seem to determine which joints of the hand are affected. Data from several sources

Occupational group	Site of osteoarthritis
Miners	Knees, spine
Furnacemen	Elbows
Ballet dancers	Feet, ankles
Footballers	Knees
Mill workers	Hands
Farmers	Hips

a joint that is immobile never gets OA as can be seen in patients who may have lost the use of their legs during childhood; while they may get OA in their arms, they never get it in the joints of their legs. Another extremely important factor seems to be the genetic predisposition, and in identical twin studies Spector has shown that for OA of the knee, this is far and away the most significant determinant of the disease.[2]

Age is an important factor and the prevalence of OA increases very significantly with age; by the age of 70 almost everyone has at least one joint affected by the disease. The effect of sex is such that OA is slightly more common in females than in males, and there are also some differences in the expression of the disease in different races. Weight — or to be precise, excess weight — is related to OA in interesting ways.[3] Many epidemiological studies have shown that OA of the knee is positively associated with obesity. This is not surprising as it seems reasonable to suppose that the stress through the joint is likely to be greater in the obese than the slim. OA of the hip, by contrast, shows only a weak association with increasing weight which is a rather counter-intuitive result. The other important association is between obesity and OA of the hand. No very convincing explanation for this association has been put forward and it certainly cannot be anything to do with body weight *per se*; the most likely explanation is that it may reflect some metabolic abnormality which leads to both the increase in body weight and the development of OA.

Damage to joints predisposes them to developing OA and if a fracture line extends into a joint, then the joint invariably contracts the disease some years later. The knee is particularly at risk from developing OA secondary to trauma and any accident which damages the cartilages or the cruciate ligaments within the joint is very likely to lead to OA.

The most generally accepted explanation of the development of OA is that various of the precipitating factors act, either together on in concert, to produce the series of changes within a joint which lead to the condition which we refer to as OA in those who have the appropriate genetic disposition.

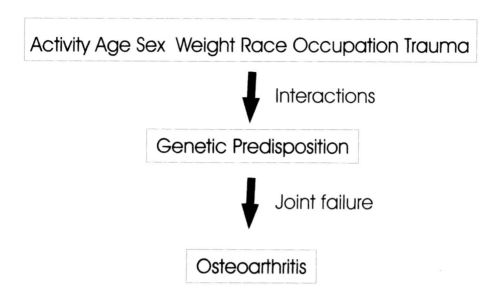

3   *Model of development of osteoarthritis. Interactions between the various precipitants act in those with the necessary genetic predisposition produces joint failure, recognised as osteoarthritis*

So, let us suppose that occupation and OA are so intimately related that the former can be predicted from the latter. Imagine for a moment that you find yourself in the rheumatology clinic of your local hospital and that there are forty or so patients waiting to be seen. We will assume that they all have OA and your task is to find out what their occupations are. You are allowed to ask each patient which joints are affected and you can also see any x-rays they may have had taken. In how many cases would you expect to get the right answer? If the clinic were in a rural area, you might be lucky and guess that one or two were farmers, especially if you said that they were *all* farmers, but this would be cheating and is not permitted under the rules of the contest. In a city hospital, it is not likely that *any* of the patients would be farmers, whether or not they had OA of the hip.

I would like to put any money on the fact that you would not be able to determine *any* of the occupations of the living patients on the basis of the distribution of their OA. The likelihood of even getting the right answer by chance can easily be shown to be very slim indeed. The probability of getting the right answer depends upon the number of individuals in any particular occupation divided by the number of people in the total workforce. For example, if there were 350 farmers in the workforce served by the clinic at which you carry out your experiment, and the total number of workers in all occupations is 60,000, then the probability of guessing correctly would be slightly less than 0.6% or one chance in about 160. You could easily calculate the odds of guessing correctly if you knew both numbers in the sum, but you will see that it would not be possible to calculate the probability of guessing the correct occupation of an individual from a skeletal assemblage by chance since both numbers required for the calculation are not and never can be known.

If you agree that you would not be able to determine occupation from the site or sites of OA in modern patients, how much better do you think that you would be able to do in the case of skeletons?

Those who consider that they possess this almost mystical ability will sometimes appeal to Sherlock Holmes and his supposed skill at inferring great matters from small details to support them. 'And the murderer?' (asks Inspector Lestrade). 'Is a tall man, left-handed, limps with the right leg, wears thick-soled shooting-boots and a grey cloak, smokes Indian cigars, used a cigar-holder, and carries a blunt pen-knife in his pocket,' replies Holmes without hesitation.[4] The fallacy in appealing to Holmes is that Conan Doyle *knew* what the answers were before he put the words into Holmes's mouth, and his predictions were therefore never put to the test; Holmes was in the enviable position that he could *never* be wrong (unless Conan Doyle wanted him to be for dramatic effect) since, in effect, he knew the answer in advance. In real life, the correctness or otherwise of predictions or inferences must be verified, usually by some experimental procedure. To refer back to our earlier thought experiment, the only way to find out whether or not your determination of occupation was correct would be to ask the patient; this is the chosen method of most doctors, and very few rely on Holmes's methods!

There is another objection to using OA as a means to predict occupation from the skeleton and this is what might be called a directional problem. Suppose that we have a skeleton from a Neolithic context with OA of the elbows, knees and toes. The skeleton is female and so we conclude that she spent her time grinding corn in a quern; we say this because we know that using a quern involves kneeling with toes bent and much flexing and extending at the elbows. Refer back to figure **3**, however, and you will see that there are several factors, including occupation, which may cause OA. No matter what the antecedents, however, the end result is the same — osteoarthritis. By analogy, consider a bucket of water which you are told has been filled by one or more of five taps (**4**). How would you be able to tell which of the taps was (or were) the source of water in the bucket? The answer is, of course, that you could not possibly do so. And the same is true of OA. Faced with a skeleton with OA it is absolutely impossible to state which of the precipitants was responsible. In this situation we are facing the wrong direction; we need to be at the tap end, and not the bucket end.

An argument which could be made against my contention is that it is that the assignment of occupation is based on the pattern of OA and that different occupations involve the use of different joints which are thereby induced to develop OA. The *pattern* of OA is then used to infer the occupation — backwards, as it were. It is not difficult to show that even this method is seriously flawed, however.

The error is due to the fact that none of the supposed varieties of occupational OA is site specific. I have alluded to this fact before. The strongest and most reliable relationship seems to be between farming and OA of the hip, but not everyone who has OA of the hip is a farmer, and indeed, under most circumstances, farmers will be in a minority of those

4 *Model of osteoarthritis. The five taps empty into the beaker below, but from an examination of the water it will not be possible to determine which tap(s) provided the water. From a study of a joint with osteoarthritis it will not be possible to determine which of the precipitants was responsible*

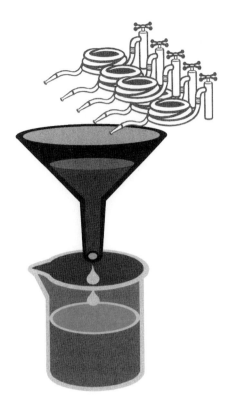

with this disease. Imagine then that in a large skeletal assemblage there are 10 skeletons with OA of the hip. How can you possibly tell which is a farmer? You can't, and nor can anyone else. What bedevils all this kind of work — deducing anything about an individual from his or her skeletal morphology — is that there is no way in which the results of speculation can be validated. It is simply not possible to ask your subject what his occupation was; it is possible that you will be right by chance — although you cannot calculate the probability of being correct — but you will never be sure.

In some cases, inferences about the activities of individual skeletons are made using ethnographic information as a guide. For example, Merbs carried out a very detailed analysis of Inuit skeletons, noting the pathology in each and then relating the pathology to the kinds of tasks which he assumed were being undertaken on the basis of observations in more recent groups of Inuits who had been observed at work.[5] Thus he was able to speculate which individuals had carried out which tasks. The study was painstakingly carried out but there exists no way to verify the conclusions unless it can be shown that those, and only those, who carry out particular tasks develop a peculiar kind of pathology. I know of no study in which this has been shown to be the case; I am sure that certain kinds of OA might be found to be associated with some work practices, but we then come back to the problem discussed in the previous paragraph. Only if particular occupations are associated uniquely with a certain type of disease can the disease be securely attributed to the occupation.

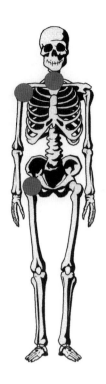
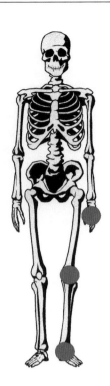

5   *Patterns of osteoarthritis in two hypothetical populations. In the one on the left (A), the disease affects the cervical spine, shoulder and hip; in that on the right (B), the hand, knee and foot are affected*

Very occasionally, skeletons are found in coffins to which the coffin plate is still attached and which gives the name of the incumbent, age at death and so on. Sometimes the occupation is put on the coffin plate, but even when this is omitted, it may be possible to find it from documentary sources. Where this can be done, one can examine the relationship between OA and occupation using conventional epidemiological methods.

I have mentioned the Spitalfields crypt before. It was used for burial between 1729 and 1869, and 968 skeletons were recovered from it of which 367 had legible coffin plates which gave the name of the individual contained in the coffin. Each of the skeletons was examined to determine the presence and distribution of OA, and occupations were obtained from a variety of historical sources, of which the London trade directories were the most useful. Death certification was introduced in 1837 and so for those individuals who died after that date, occupation could be obtained from the death certificate.

Many Huguenots were living in the area at the time and they were mainly engaged in weaving. We decided to test whether there was an association between weaving and OA of the hands — one of the associations found in modern working groups.[6] In fact, none was found, nor were those engaged in *any* kind of manual work more likely to have OA of the

6   *Spine with marked scoliosis. The spine has two curves, one to the left and one to the right. This is almost certainly an idiopathic lesion*

hands than those in non-manual occupations. We also examined the relationship between occupation and OA of the spine; in this case those in *non-manual* occupations were more likely to have OA of the spine than manual workers. Why this should have been the case was not clear, although one possibility is that those who developed OA of the spine as the result of heavy work may have chosen to find something which was less physically demanding.[7] On the basis of this study, we would have been seriously in error had we said that anyone with OA of the hands had been a weaver.

Although the pattern of OA will tell you nothing about the activities of individuals, it may be more informative when considering populations as a whole. In figure **5** I have shown the pattern of OA in two hypothetical populations. In the first the disease is found most frequently in the cervical spine, shoulder and hip, whereas in the second it is found most often in the hand, knee and foot. To explain these differences we need to consider which of the precipitating factors (see **3**) might be involved. Of these, weight (and, by inference, nutrition) and activity seem to be the only plausible possibilities since we can control for any differences in age and sex statistically, race does not enter into our considerations, and genetic factors will not have changed in the short time involved. Of the two possibilities, differences in types of activity have to be seriously considered and would probably be the most significant determinant of the patterns seen. Even so, we may not be able to say *what* kinds of activities were causative, but it is at least a start to say that the pattern of activity between the two populations differed.

Determining occupation from other types of pathology

Other types of pathology are not very often used to infer occupation but there is one example — involving Calvin Wells — which is worth describing. In 1967 he reported on a group of 50 burials which had been recovered from the church of St Michael-at-Thorn in Norwich. Only eight of the burials had well-preserved spines and among these there were three with spinal deformities, two (both female) with scoliosis and one (a male) with kyphosis. Both conditions are forms of spinal curvature; in scoliosis the curvature is from side to side whereas in kyphosis it is from front to back. Finding two of eight spines with scoliosis is remarkable and it prompted Wells to seek an explanation in the presumed occupations of the women by — as he put it — 'the integration of informed speculation based upon a wide experience of bone pathology with information gleaned from the contemporary art of the period and ancient city records'.[8]

Wells noted that for centuries Norwich had been a centre of weaving and he supposed that the two women with scoliosis had been employed as weavers and that this had been the cause of their deformity. (The man with kyphosis Wells decided had not been a weaver but a tailor, his deformity arising from his habit of sitting cross-legged, hunched over his work.) Even supposing that Wells was correct in his assumptions, and there is no hard evidence to support him, a much more likely explanation of this unusual cluster of cases is that the two women had gravitated towards Norwich, since disadvantaged individuals generally tend to go to large centres of population where they may be better able to support themselves by begging or other means. Recently Ann Stirland has found another unusual cluster of cases of scoliosis in a skeletal group from the church of St Margaret in Madgalen Street in Norwich (16 cases among 368 adults). The cemetery of St Margaret's was used from 1240-1468 and was the poorest medieval church in the parish. Stirland's finding lends further support to the view that those who were disadvantaged in some way moved to the city.[9]

On this occasion, it seems that Wells's wide experience of bone pathology let him down. There are some congenital causes of scoliosis but in most cases, the cause is unknown — idiopathic in the medical jargon, and most cases appear after puberty. There is little reason to suppose that Wells's cases were not of the normal idiopathic type; certainly, there are no modern clinical data which would link the condition with any kind of occupation.

4 Populations at large

Reporting interesting single cases of disease or anatomical anomalies is a time honoured way of proceeding for BS and has its value, but the most useful information is obtained from considering populations of skeletons, in fact from the use of epidemiological methods. These may vary from the presentation of the age and sex distribution of the assemblage, to calculating the prevalence of disease or testing hypotheses; in this chapter I will stick to a discussion of the first two of these, and those who wish to learn about testing hypotheses and other epidemiological methods will find these matters explored in detail elsewhere.[1]

Demography

When presenting the results of their study of a skeletal assemblage, BS will always show the age and sex distribution of the skeletons (the demography) of the assemblage they have examined. In modern demography, the distribution of age at death by sex can provide important information about the overall health of the population, and the state of development of the society can also be inferred. In societies where sanitation and nutrition are poor, there is a high infant and child mortality rate, but those who survive through childhood may expect to survive into relative old age. Thus, if the numbers of deaths are plotted by age, the result is a U-shaped curve, with the majority of deaths at both extremes of age. As hygiene and nutrition improve, and as medical services start to make their influence felt, the number of deaths in infancy in childhood decreases and the death curve changes shape; the left-hand arm of the U-shaped curve is pushed down and the right arm tends to rise (**7**). The expectation is that if the shape of the mortality curve is derived from a sufficiently large skeletal assemblage, we may be able to say something about the state of development of the population from which the assemblage was drawn.

The state of preservation of most assemblages, however, means inevitably that not all the skeletons will be given an age and/or a sex; as we have seen earlier, none of the sub-adults will be given a sex although they will be given a more precise age than the adults. As a result, when the ages and sexes are tabulated, the result will be something like that shown in **Table 3**; these are the results for burials from a Black Death cemetery in London. The question arises as how to plot the results? Plotting the numbers is not very helpful for comparative purposes, since comparisons are best made with proportions. If

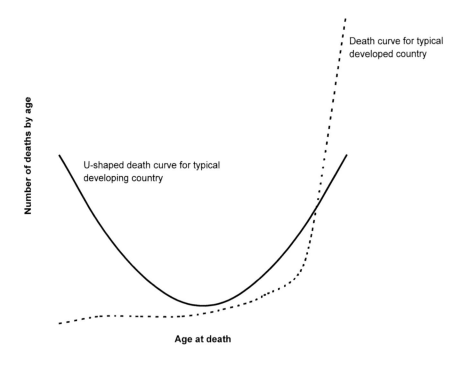

7   *Typical death curves in a developing and a developed country. In the developing country, the majority of deaths occur at both extremes of life; in the developed country, there are few deaths among the young and the great majority of deaths occur in old age*

Table 3   Sex and age distribution of burials from a plague pit in London. N = 600

Age	Male	Female	Unknown sex
Infant			68
Juvenile			109
15-	21	24	9
25-	48	45	6
35-	45	24	2
45+	48	24	
Adult	48	50	27
Unknown			2
Total	210	167	223

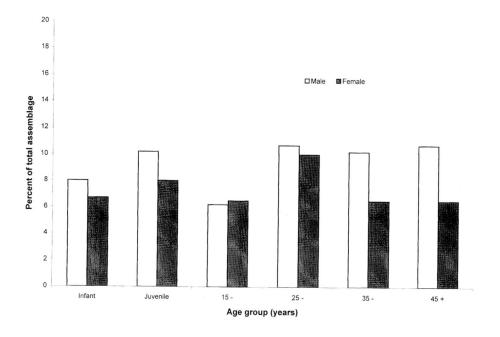

8   *Age and sex distribution of skeletal assemblage from a plague pit in London after correction factors have been applied. For description of corrections factors, see text*

the proportions of deaths at each age are to be plotted, what number is to be used in the denominator? Surely not the total number of skeletons in the assemblage, since some of those in the denominator will not appear in the numerator — although I have seen this done. The usual approach in modern demography is to show deaths at each age as a proportion of the total number of deaths for each sex separately, so this is what we will do here. But this raises two further problems: should the proportions be given only for those skeletons to which an age can be given, or should *all* those with an assignment of sex be used? The result of using these two approaches is shown in figure **8**; increasing the value of the numerator causes the proportion dying at each age to decrease. But we still have not accounted for the sub-adults who represent very nearly a third of all the bodies in the cemetery. Clearly some means must be found to do this and one way is to allocate skeletons of unknown age or sex using the following assumptions:

  • the sex ratio of the sub-adults is the same as that of the adults

  • the adults of unknown age are evenly distributed throughout each of the age classes

Some BS might object to the last point on the grounds that skeletons of the elderly are more prone to post mortem damage because they are more likely to have pathological

Table 4 Sex and age distribution of burials from a plague pit in London after application
of correction factors. For details see text. N = 600

Age	Male	Female
Infant	48	40
Juvenile	61	48
15-	37	39
25-	64	60
35-	61	39
45+	64	39
Total	335	223

change. There seems no way to test this notion since we cannot know the state of
skeletons which do not survive and so we will ignore that objection and proceed.

The male/female ratio for the deaths from the plague pit was 1.25:1 and the infants and
juveniles can be re-allocated by sex accordingly. The 48 males and 50 females of unknown
age can be equally distributed between the four adult age classes. Next the 27 adults of
unknown sex can be allocated between the age and sex classes by first applying the sex ratio
and then distributing the resultant males and females equally between the age classes; there
is nothing which can be done about the two fragmentary skeletons to which neither age nor
sex could be attributed and they have to be discarded from further consideration. When all
the sums are done, the numbers of males and females of each age group is as shown in
Table 4. Now, when these figures are used to construct the graph of proportional mortality,
we find that the trend we observed before has continued, that is, the proportion of those
dying in adulthood has decreased still further. It will be noted, however, that the shape of
the graph approximates to neither of the curves shown in figure **7**. This is unfortunately
almost always the case with assemblages of skeletons, and to understand why this might be
we need to consider the samples with which BS have to deal.

The nature of the assemblage

Assemblages such as the one from the plague pit are unusual in as much as they derive
from natural disasters which can be dated to within quite narrow limits. Most burial
grounds are used for very many years — centuries as a rule — and the inhabitants of a
cemetery are a social rather than a biological population and subject to what might be
called the law of diminishing numbers (**9**). Almost nothing about a burial assemblage is
random, and randomness is the very essence of modern epidemiology; epidemiology is
the study of populations and BS often find themselves in the position of M. Jourdain, who
did not realise that he had been speaking prose all his life — *they* do not realise that they

have been practising epidemiology all their lives.

The place where one is buried is determined by social factors, and this was especially true in the past when individuals may seldom have left their own parish and were buried within it, except in rather unusual circumstances. Once buried, the forces of decay and decomposition start to work on the body. These are not very well understood but are known to depend to a large extent on the characteristics of the medium in which the body is buried; under waterlogged, anaerobic conditions, for example, decomposition will proceed much more slowly than in a dry, well aerated soil. Eventually the soft tissues will disappear, leaving the skeleton, which is itself subject to decay and disturbance. Small animals may burrow into a burial and either disturb or remove bones, and old burials are disturbed by the grave diggers to make way for new ones. Disturbance of burials was sometimes accidental when they were unmarked, but it was also customary at some times and in some places, deliberately to dig up bones and remove them to a charnel house, or to a crypt so that there would be room for newcomers. How well bones survive if they are undisturbed also depends upon the soil conditions; generally they will survive poorly in a wet, acid soil, much better in a dry, alkaline soil. There are factors in the micro-environment, however, which must also be as important as in any cemetery: a well-preserved skeleton may be found right next to one which has been almost disintegrated. The plan of any cemetery will illustrate this very well; whole skeletons, skeletons without heads, pairs of legs, a few limb bones, these all appear (**10**) and we can be sure that the processes are not random. Cemeteries will fall out of use and be forgotten. If the land which they once occupied is built on, this may also disturb some of the burials, and also restrict the area of the cemetery which can be excavated. When the time comes for excavation, the

Original cemetery population

Decay and decomposition

Disturbance

Excavation

Final assemblage

9 Model to show effects of diminishing numbers (as shown by successive loss of colour) of individuals in a cemetery

archaeologist will perforce be restricted to the area which is not covered by buildings, and an unknown number of burials will be unavailable. Further losses may occur during excavation, subsequent washing and despatch to and from the BS's laboratory. The assemblage which is finally examined and reported on is but a fraction of the total number

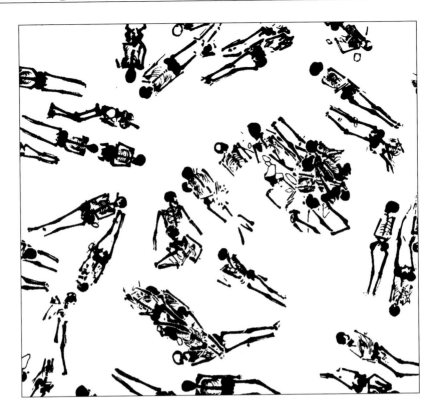

10 Excavation plan of cemetery showing skeletons in various stages of preservation

originally contained within the cemetery, and its relationship to the living population of which it was once a part is problematic.

There seems to be no way accurately to determine how great the rate of attrition is and what proportion of the original cemetery population ends up on the BS's bench, even when a complete cemetery is excavated as sometimes happens when a parish church has fallen out of use, for example. Indeed, there is probably *no* way in which it can be done. The BS, therefore, has to use a sample which is markedly flawed from the epidemiological point of view, but as there is nothing which he can do to improve the situation, he must either proceed regardless or take up some other academic endeavour. What he — and the readers of his papers, or the listeners to his papers — must do, however, is to be circumspect about the conclusions he draws from his studies. Hedging around, and peppering prose with 'ifs' and 'buts', does not usually make for an exciting read; it is much more refreshing to read firm, definite conclusions and this is no doubt why the interpretive school of bone studies is more often compelling than the agnostic. But interesting or not, readers and listeners might do well occasionally to ask the author how he has validated his conclusions — but don't expect that you will always get a very convincing answer.

The frequency of disease

It is useful to be able to compare the frequency of disease between populations which may be separated either by time or space. There are two ways in which the frequency of a disease is expressed, its incidence and its prevalence. The incidence of a disease is the number of new cases which arise in a population at risk over a defined period; the prevalence is the proportion of the study population which has the disease of interest. Incidence is generally expressed as so many cases per thousand or hundred thousand of the population per year — or whatever time base is appropriate for the disease under consideration (it will be long for a chronic condition, short for an acute one). Thus

$$\text{Incidence} = n/N \div t$$

where n = number of new cases, N = total population at risk and t = time period.

Incidence is a true rate since it has a time base and it is important to note that the population at risk *excludes* those who already have the disease. So, for example, if the incidence of measles in pre-school children were to be determined, a suitable study group would be formed and the number of those who contracted measles over the study period — say a month — would be noted. The study group, however, would *exclude* any child who had measles at the start of the study period because, by definition, they could not be at risk of contracting it.

Prevalence is a simple proportion:

$$\text{Prevalence} = n/N$$

where n = total number of cases and N = total number in study population.

Although prevalence is not a true rate because it does not have a time base, it is a long established custom to refer to it as a rate and there is no likelihood that this habit will be broken in the foreseeable future.

There is a relationship between incidence and prevalence such that

$$P \approx I \times D$$

where P = prevalence, I = incidence, and D = duration of disease.

The prevalence and incidence of the acute diseases of childhood, such as measles, are roughly equal because the duration of the illness is short. On the other hand, the prevalence of chronic diseases, such as osteoarthritis, is much greater than the incidence — sometimes much greater — because they have a long natural history.

The important thing to note is that the only measure of disease frequency which can be applied to skeletal assemblages is prevalence, as it is impossible to count *new* cases of disease. Despite this obvious conclusion from what has gone before, many BS persist in using incidence when describing the frequency of disease in their assemblages; some may even talk about infant mortality rates, based on the number of infants found in the group of skeletons. When you see that the infant mortality rate (IMR) is calculated as

$$IMR = \text{Number of deaths in first year} \div \text{Total number of live births}$$

it will be immediately obvious that it is a statistic which could never be applied to a skeletal population since the denominator is unknown. When BS refer to an infant mortality rate — or indeed to any other rate — they are actually referring to a proportion; in the case of the IMR, they are referring to the proportion of infants in the assemblage, and this will bear little or no relationship to the magnitude of the IMR.

The prevalence of diseases can be calculated in skeletal populations and there are ways in which it can be validly compared between populations as explained elsewhere.[2] It is also possible to slightly refine the method by calculating age- and sex-specific prevalences. The reason for doing this is that if the expression of a disease is age or sex dependent, then the so-called crude prevalence (the one obtained using the total population in the denominator) may be distorted by the structure of the population under study. For example, the prevalence of OA increases markedly with age and comparing the crude prevalence of a population composed mainly of young people with one composed mainly of the elderly would show that OA was more common in the older population. Not very surprising. Using age-specific prevalence, however, might show that OA was actually more common among the younger members of the 'young' population, and this would be a more interesting finding.

The prevalence of OA has been studied in most detail because this is by far the most common disease found in the skeleton and so BS have relatively large numbers to play with. Studies have shown that, in the past, OA largely behaved according to modern expectations; that is, it is slightly more common in females than in males and the prevalence increases greatly with age. The prevalence rates are not directly comparable with modern day rates, but rates in different assemblages can be compared using the appropriate techniques and it has been found that the expression of the disease has changed slightly over time. Before about 1500, OA of the hip was more common that OA of the knee, whereas after that date, and continuing to the present day, the converse is true. The other change which has been noted concerns OA of the hands. In earlier times it was most usual for the disease to affect only a single joint in the hands, whereas in the post-medieval period it was more likely that more than one joint would be affected.[3]

Like so much else that occurs in the skeleton, it is not clear what has caused these changes although it may be of some significance that the changes have affected both joints in which there is a clear association between OA and obesity and perhaps the answer is to be found in alterations in nutrition or the diet. The other likely explanation is that there has been some persistent change in patterns of activity and these have resulted in the disease expressing itself variably over time. It is not to be excluded either that some presently unknown environmental factor is responsible. The expression of the rheumatic diseases varies by country, and in some countries between urban and rural populations, and environmental factors have been suggested as one possible cause for these differences.[4]

Expectation of life and life tables

There is, naturally, a good deal of curiosity about the life span of our ancestors and we tend to assume that life was, if not nasty and brutish, then at least short. BS examine life span by one or other of two means, estimating mean age at death and by the construction of life tables. Relying on either, however, represents a real triumph of hope over experience.

Mean age at death

The mean age at death is greatly influenced by the number of those who die at either extreme of life, as can easily be demonstrated by use of the data in **Table 5**. In the table I have shown the ages of death for two small populations, A and B, each of 20 people. The mean age at death of A is 32.1 years and of B, 34.3 years, suggesting that B has a better expectation of life. A look at **Table 6**, however, soon gives the lie to that notion, for whereas a quarter of all those in A reach at least the age of 60 before death, none of those from B do. The reason that the mean age at death in A seems low is that there is a much greater number of deaths at a very young age. The first few years of life are extremely hazardous and so if we calculate the mean age of death for those who survived beyond the age of five, we find that for A this is 41.9 years and for B, 36 years. This seems to accord better with what the simple examination of **Table 5** tells us and one the whole, we would probably have rather belonged to population A than to B.

Table 5 Age structure of two hypothetical skeletal assemblages

A	B
1	1
1	8
2	10
3	11
4	15
7	24
9	30
11	32
19	36
20	37
28	37
37	38
48	40
55	45
58	48
60	49
67	50
69	57
70	58
71	59

Table 6 Number of individuals of two hypothetical skeletal assemblages in age categories

Age range	A	B
0-	4	1
5-	3	1
10-	2	3
20-	3	7
40-	3	8
60+	5	0

Whatever its defects, calculating the mean age of a population of skeletons at least seems to be a simple procedure, but there is one procedural matter which has to be considered. We have already seen how difficult it is to give anything like a precise age to an adult skeleton and that the best we are likely to be able to do is to express the age within five- or ten-year age bands; with children we can do considerably better and get to within a year or two of the 'true' age. If we refer back to **Table 4**, where we see that the ages of the adults is expressed in three ten-year bands and a final open-ended category of 45+. Now what age are we going to use when calculating the mean age at death? Assuming that our ascertainment of age is so good that the ages of the adult really do lie within the bounds we have suggested, within each ten-year age band the individual ages will vary between, let's say, 20 and 29 years, and we have no way of knowing how they are spread. Some BS use the lower bound in their calculations — everyone is assumed to be 20, or 30, and so on — and this will tend to lower the apparent mean. A more defensible method is to use the mid-point of each range; thus all individuals in the 20-29 age group would be considered to have been 25 years at death. This method cannot be used for the final group which has no upper limit. We do not know how far this extends; some BS add more age groups — 45-54, 55-64 and so on — but unless the age groups are extended to absurd lengths, there will come some point at which an open-ended age category has to be employed. Using a large number of age groups when ageing adults, particularly if they are five-year categories, does nothing but give a spurious impression of accuracy to methods which are inherently inaccurate. Whatever the lower bound of the last open-ended age category, we have no idea what the upper bound is. Is it 60, 70, 80, 90? And since we do not know, we cannot use the mid-point to calculate mean age at death unless we arbitrarily decide on an upper bound. We may assume, for example, that no one in the population with which we are dealing will live beyond the age of 70, and fix this as the upper bound.

Apart from being an inherently poor measure for comparing the mortality experience of different populations, the mean age of a skeletal population will almost certainly be at best a serious underestimate of the actual mean age. Where BS purport to be able to detect a difference in mean age between skeletal groups of a year or two, or where the result is expressed to several places of decimals, reach for a novel.

Life tables

A better approach to the problem of expectation of life is to disregard means altogether and base the estimates on life tables. The production of a life table requires a lot a number crunching, but the principle underlying it is straightforward. The life table is constructed from the age-specific death rates of the population being studied. For the population of England and Wales for 1950, for example, it would be necessary to know the number of individuals alive in each age group during the year and the number dying in the year; the death rate is then simply calculated for each age-class, usually composed of single years; each sex is considerably separately, of course.

Table 7 Life table prepared from data for England and Wales.
l_x = number alive at year x; d_x = number dying in year x;
p_x = probability of surviving to year $x+1$; q_x = probability of dying in year x;
e_x = expectation of life at year x. Note that $p_x + q_x$ must equal 1

Age x	l_x	d_x	p_x	q_x	e_x
0	100,000	1,271	0.98729	0.01271	71.0
1	98,729	84	0.99915	0.00085	71.0
2	98,645	51	0.99948	0.00052	70.0
3	98,594	36	0.99962	0.00038	69.1
4	98,557	•	•	•	
•		•	•	•	
•		•	•	•	
•		•	•	•	
50	92,758	•	•	•	24.3
•		•	•	•	
•		•	•	•	
•		•	•	•	
85	14,152	•	•	•	4.3
•		•	•	•	
•		•	•	•	
100	165	•	•	•	1.9

To construct the life table, the death rates obtained from the real population are applied to a hypothetical one of 100,000 individuals aged less than one year of age. From the death rate one can calculate how many of the original 100,000 individuals died in their first year; this number is deducted from the base number to find how many survived into the second year. This procedure is continued for all ages until no one is left. From the resulting table, a number of statistics can be derived; including the probability of dying from one year to the next (denoted as q_x), the probability of surviving from one year to the next (p_x), and the expectation life at a particular age (e_x). An extract of a life table is shown in **Table 7** based on death rates on males in England and Wales.

A different technique has to be applied to the construction of a life table based on skeletal ages at death since we have no mortality data to guide us. In this case, the ages at death assigned to the skeletons are put into the 'Age' column and a new column is introduced, D_x, the number of skeletons in each age class; d_x is the proportion of skeletons in each age class, l_x, the probability of surviving into the next age class, q_x is the probability of death, and e_x is the expectation of life for each age class. A life table prepared from archaeological data is shown in **Table 8**. Expectation of life is calculated from d_x by adding up all the years contributed by the different proportions of the assemblage and

Table 8 Life table constructed from data derived from Boddington (op cit).

D_x = number in each age group; d_x = proportion in each age group;
l_x = proportion apparently surviving to next age group;
q_x = probability of death in each age group;
e_x = expectation of life at each age group

Age x	D_x	d_x	l_x	q_x	e_x
0	66	21.1	100.0	0.21	21.8
1	7	2.1	79.9	0.03	24.5
2	35	10.7	77.8	0.14	24.2
6	32	9.8	67.1	0.15	23.7
12	11	3.4	57.3	0.06	21.2
17	57	17.3	53.9	0.32	17.4
25	45	13.7	36.6	0.37	15.7
35	32	9.8	22.9	0.43	12.2
45	43	13.1	13.1	1.00	7.5

dividing by 100. The number of years considered to have lived is the mid-point of the age range; thus for the first row, the years contributed is calculated as 21.2 x 0.5 = 33 years since it is assumed that all those dying between 0 and 1 year lived, on average, half-a-year — almost certainly a considerable overestimate. Those dying between the ages of 1 and 2 contributed on average 1.5 years, so the total contribution is 2.1 x 1.5 = 3.15 years. Similar considerations are applied to each row and the total number of years is derived and the supposed expectation of life at year 0 can be calculated. For the final age category, some decision has be made about what the upper bound is; for the example shown, the author decided on the age of 60.[5]

Some important points need to be taken into account when reviewing the results obtained from archaeological life tables, the most obvious being that it relies entirely on the estimate of age at death and — as we have seen — this is problematic to say the least for adults.[6] Values of e_x may appear to be accurate if they are expressed to one or more places of decimals, but appearances are spurious since the calculation of e_x is only as accurate as the underlying estimate of age at death. It is a common trick to denote accuracy by expressing statistics to several places of decimals; the accuracy of a derived statistic is only that of the data on which the calculation was based and it is always worthwhile taking a glance at the raw data before relying too much on derived data. No amount of manipulation can improve the quality of flawed data although it is commonly thought otherwise, especially if they are made to pass through a computer; remember, however, rubbish in, rubbish out.

Another difficulty with archaeological life tables is that the population is neither complete nor non-random; it is also an accumulation of skeletons over perhaps several hundred years and, as suggested above, we have no true idea of what proportion it represents of the total number of individual buried in the cemetery. Nor is any attempt made to deal with individuals to whom an age cannot be assigned, and this may be a substantial proportion of the total.

Finally — and this is not a critique of life tables *per se* — the life expectation derived is a mean obtained from many different populations who lived during the period over which the cemetery was used. The very long periods which generally have to be applied to epidemiological or demographic data result in much detail being lost; the expectation of life for a burial assemblage which covers 300-400 years is the mean expectation of life over the whole period, during which it may have fluctuated considerably.

Whatever may be said to the contrary, the calculation of life tables based on the ageing of skeletons will give an inaccurate impression of expectation of life and, unfortunately, the magnitude of the error cannot be estimated and therefore corrected. One cannot but have the greatest sympathy with those who bid farewell to archaeological demography.[7] And even though this view was robustly rebutted, it seems clear — to this author at least — on which side of the argument the truth lies.

Part 2: Death

5 What did our remote ancestors die of?

You are a doctor; imagine that you have a time machine and could transport yourself back to the Palaeolithic or Mesolithic — what diseases do you suppose you would have to deal with, and what would be the causes of death? We are dealing with hunter-gatherers who went around in bands of 40-60, and who most consider died in their 30s. Since there are so few hunter-gatherer remains to examine to get answers to our questions, we need to consider other lines of evidence, including that derived from the study of wild primates and modern hunter-gatherers.

Evidence from modern hunter-gatherers is not entirely reliable since their way of life must be different in many respects from that of our ancestors of several thousand years ago, but they seem to suffer rather little from chronic diseases such as heart disease or hypertension, at least until they come into contact with or adopt a western diet and lifestyle. The effects of alterations in a traditional diet, drinking alcohol and smoking all wreak havoc, however, and many indigenous peoples are turning their backs on what we like to refer to as civilisation and are re-learning their original way of life.[1]

Under natural conditions, animals suffer from a high death rate between (and including) birth and puberty and in old age. In the between years, the number of deaths is low, unless the animal is hunted, but man has never had any natural predators and deaths from predation can be ruled out. Females would have been prone to death from the complications of pregnancy and on this account, the death rate among young females would probable have been higher than among young males. A difficult labour, with the foetus impacted, a uterine tear or a placenta praevia with catastrophic bleeding, would have been among the conditions likely to end in the death of the mother and in most cases, of the foetus also.

In the past, males had an easier life than females — some may argue that this applies still — but on their relatively infrequent hunting trips, some of the males would have sustained injuries, some inflicted by their prey, others from trips and falls. Some, such as a compound fracture of the leg would have been fatal as a result of blood loss or infection, but simple fractures could be survived so long as there was a reasonably well-developed social network to ensure that the injured man was cared for while he recovered. Primates in the wild fracture limbs in falls and the limbs heal well and in some cases it is certain that the animal has lived for many months after the injury since it has developed secondary osteoarthritis in the joints of the affected limb. Modern orthopaedic teaching has it that it is important to immobilise a fractured limb if it is to heal, but animals in the wild are unable to do this and it is doubtful whether hunter-gatherers had any knowledge about splinting, so there may have been a high prevalence of poorly healed fractures. If this were the case, and if the consequence was that mobility was greatly impaired, then the injured man would have been unlikely to survive.

Hunter-gatherer bands were nomadic, wandering from place to place, the sites where they settled being determined by the availability of water, game and sources of fruit and vegetables. In the northern winters they would of necessity had to shelter during periods of bad weather and one can imagine that food supplies would have dwindled and they may well have suffered from scurvy (lack of vitamin C) at such times but most would have been able to survive until food became more plentiful. There would have been times of starvation, of course, and in times of severe drought, dehydration and death would have been likely.

The hunter-gatherers would not have much contact with other bands although there may have been some skirmishing at territorial boundaries and it is hard to believe that fights did not break out from time to time and that injuries — trivial and severe — would have been sustained. Nor can violence within the band be ignored; sickly and weak infants may well have been either left to die or have actually been put to death. And adolescent boys would have been as likely to fight over girls and other matters in the same way as they do nowadays. Skin and flesh wounds may have become infected, but we tend to forget that healing took place before the antibiotic era. Deep flesh wounds would be more likely to become infected than surface wounds and any uncontained infection could lead to very serious complications, including septicaemia which would have been fatal. Penetrating wounds contaminated with soil bacteria would lead to the possibility of tetanus and this infection would have been invariably fatal. I have mentioned the possibility of sustaining fractures from accidents, but they are also a common consequence of fighting. The fractures usually involve the face and nose, but also the forearm giving rise to the so-called parry fracture. This is a fracture of the radius or ulna (or both) and is sustained when raising the forearm to protect against a blow to the head. These fractures are quite common in skeletal assemblages from more recent times, and they often fail to unite. Fractures of the skull are the most feared consequences of fighting since they may damage the underlying soft tissues. Bleeding into the skull causes the intra-cranial pressure to rise and this produces pressure on the brain which, if continued for any length of time, will interfere with the normal functioning of the vital centres in the brain stem; coma and death would then quickly supervene.

The most significant potential source of disease for our hunter-gatherers, however, would have been infectious agents and we can be absolutely certain that they harboured a variety of potential pathogens. These would have been one of three groups:

• harmless commensals

• organisms acquired during childhood from other members of the group which caused an illness of limited duration

- organisms acquired from animals by direct or indirect contact, or from intermediate hosts

Acute infections such as those common in childhood now, would have been unknown among hunter-gatherers because there were too few in the group to sustain the infection. Studies of measles, for example, have shown that the disease cannot be sustained within a community unless there are at least 3,000 cases a year and this will not occur if the population is less than about 300,000. Populations of this size were unknown before the establishment of a settled way of life and the building of towns and cities, and so measles must have appeared as a new disease about 6,000 years ago; the virus is thought to have derived from the distemper virus of dogs.

Water-borne organisms were — still are — a common source of mortality and morbidity in the past, especially where sewage and drinking water were not separated. Infantile diarrhoea is a present-day scourge in the tropics; the populations are large, there is often no safe supply of drinking water, and infants are very prone to infecting themselves by the faeco-oral route. Gastro-intestinal infections and diarrhoea must have been very common in the past and it may be that many of the infants who appear in the skeletal record died because their mothers did not know how to stop them pouring fluid from their bottoms. In the nineteenth century, the most dread water-borne disease was cholera. There were five epidemics of cholera during the century. Many thousands died in the early epidemics but in the last — in 1893 — by which time the mode of spread of the disease was understood and drinking water and sewage were separate, only 135 persons died (see **Table 9**).

The spread of disease by the faeco-oral route would have been inevitable in hunter-gatherer times but the organisms spread this way would predominantly have been intestinal parasites, both pathogenic and commensal. Both large and small parasitic organisms would be present in the bowel of our remote ancestors, all almost certainly derived from primates and other animals. Among the nematode (worm) species we would expect to find *Ascaris*, *Trichuris*, *Enterobius* and *Trichinella*, the hookworms *Ancylostoma* and *Necator*, *Stongyloides*, and tapeworms of the *Taenia* species. Single-celled organisms (protozoa) which would have inhabited the bowel would have included *Entomoeba coli*, *E. histolytica*, *Giardia lamblia*, *Iodamoeba*, *Endolimax*, *Trichomonas* and *Isospora*, and species of *Schistosoma*. Parasites evolve with their hosts so that they do them little or no damage since it ill behoves a parasite to kill the organism on which they depend for their own livelihood, and some of the parasites cited above are harmless. The hookworms, however, may cause serious disease if present in large numbers, *Strongyloides* is also pathogenic in large numbers, and *E. histolytica*, *G. lambia* and the schistosomes also produce disease — sometimes fatal disease — in their human hosts.

The importance of the spread of pathogens from animals to humans cannot be overemphasised and it occurs to the present day. Viruses spreading from primates to man may cause devastating diseases — one has only to think of the AIDS epidemic in Africa to

Table 9 Numbers dying in the great cholera outbreaks in England during the nineteenth century. The 1831 epidemic occurred before the registration of deaths became compulsory

Date of epidemic	Number of deaths
1831-2	No data available
1848-9	54,398
1853-4	24,516
1865-6	14,378
1893	135

Table 10 Derivation of some common infections from animal hosts

Disease	Animal source	Infectious agent
Common cold	Horse	Rhinovirus
Diptheria	Cattle	Related bacterium
Measles	Dog	Distemper virus
Syphilis	Monkey	Money treponemes
Tuberculosis	Cattle	*Mycobacterium bovis*
Influenza Mumps } Smallpox	Domestic animals; birds	Related viruses

realise this to be true. The earliest of the parasites were derived from other primates, but contact with other animals would have allowed the passage of parasites which were normally present in them. Pathogens would also be spread through the agency of blood sucking insects, lice and fleas. Malaria, derived originally from monkeys, could be spread through the agency of mosquitoes, and even if lice and fleas did not spread much disease, their presence would have been at the very least of nuisance value. Many other common infections are also thought to have been derived from organisms originally present in animals and the derivation of some of these is shown in **Table 10**.

The limited evidence which we have to hand gives us little indication of the causes of death of our hunter-gatherer ancestors and it is hard to understand why they should have died at so early an age as 30 or 40. The only likely candidates seem to be accidents and infectious disease, some of those perhaps newly acquired from contact with animals, especially those which they hunted. What the rates of infectious disease in hunter-gatherers were I doubt that we will know without much further research, but this is not an area of study which presently attracts very much attention.

Our human and hominid ancestors must have been infected with some particular kinds of viruses which are able to insert their own genetic material into our DNA. These are the so-called retro-viruses, a group which includes HIV, and the areas of DNA which contain this foreign DNA are referred to as human endogenous retro-viruses (HERVs). There are thousands of HERVs in the human genome and they make up about 1% of the total content of the genetic material. There have been recent suggestions that HERVs may have conferred our ancestors with resistance to retro-viral infections, thus helping them to survive.[2] On the other hand, some other authors have suggested that HERVs may actually be implicated in the production of some diseases, including some of the autoimmune diseases.[3] Whether our hunter-gatherers were actually protected by their HERVs, or whether the presence of these relics of ancestral infections actually produced diseases from which they may have died, is another matter about which we may speculate but not pronounce on with any certainty.

6 Dying naturally

The great majority of people die from diseases which arise in their soft tissues and few of these produce any signs in the skeleton. The only bone diseases which are likely to cause death are the primary bone tumours, examples of which have been found in skeletal assemblages when they are usually greeted with great enthusiasm by the BS and a paper in a learned journal. In some groups of skeletons, especially those composed largely of children and younger individuals, there may be so few signs of pathology that this sometimes induces the BS to report that the population was healthy — healthy, that is, apart from being dead!

It is disappointing that the cause of death can be established in so few individuals in the past as it would be of the greatest interest to know how patterns of mortality have changed over time. Historians are in a much more secure position in this respect, using sources such as parish records, the *Bills of Mortality* which were first published in London in 1532, and the mortality tables published after the registration of deaths became compulsory in 1837. The best the BS can do is to comment on deaths resulting from trauma — both accidental and deliberate, infectious disease, malignant disease and a small number of other conditions.

Trauma

Trauma in its various forms accounts for approximately 10% of all pathological lesions found in the skeletons and is dealt with in detail later in the book. Fractures are the most common form of trauma seen and it is possible to determine how long the individual survived after sustaining the injury. Most people seem to have recovered from their injury but where the evidence suggests otherwise, we need to consider what the ultimate cause of death would have been. With major damage to the skull there is not much difficulty. Skull fractures cause damage to the underlying blood vessels which run in the coverings of the brain, and the resulting haemorrhage raises the intra-cranial pressure, and by this effect, pressure on the brain. If the bleeding continues then the brain stem may be pushed down through the foramen magnum at the base of the skull, and the activity of the vital centres in the brain stem is impaired and death quickly supervenes. Where head injuries are particularly severe, there may be so much brain damage that death occurs immediately.

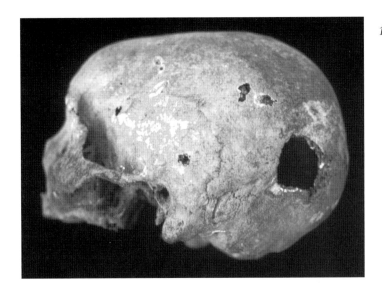

11 Skull from elderly female from eighteenth-century site in London showing several holes in the skull, almost certainly secondary deposits from a primary carcinoma of the breast

Loss of blood is an inevitable concomitant of any fracture and may vary from a trivial amount in a rib fracture to the loss of several litres in a fractured pelvis. Severe loss of blood causes clinical shock, one of the symptoms of which is thirst which would no doubt have been relieved by offering the injured man water to drink. This would actually worsen his condition as it would lead to dilution of the concentration of the electrolytes in the serum, often with disastrous consequences. In a serious accident, fractures are likely to be accompanied by soft tissue damage and death may have resulted from internal bleeding which could not have been controlled. We cannot know from the skeleton how much soft tissue injury was sustained during an accident, but there is no reason to suppose that it is different in any important respect from that seen in modern accident and emergency departments.

Malignant disease

Where we find evidence of malignant disease in the skeleton, we can safely assume that it was the cause of death. Malignant disease of the skeleton may be either primary or secondary. Primary bone tumours are rare; in the present day, they account for about 0.04% of the total number of deaths. The majority of deaths from primary bone tumours occur in young people, but there is another peak of death in later life as a complication of Paget's disease. Secondary bone tumours are more common and are the result of spread from a primary site elsewhere in the body. By no means all soft tissue tumours spread to bone. Those that most commonly involve the skeleton include carcinoma of the breast, lung and prostate, and some bones are much more likely to be involved than others. The most common skeletal sites for secondary tumours to occur are, in rank order, the vertebrae, pelvis, femur (especially the hip) and skull; secondary tumours in the upper limb are comparatively rare. The pattern of involvement is more or less the same whatever the primary, although some carcinomas do show a predilection for specific sites, carcinoma of the prostate for the pelvis, for example.

As will be explained later, most secondary tumours show themselves as holes in the bone, but carcinoma of the prostate causes the production of new bone, most usually within the bone so that an affected bone may appear normal and the tumour discovered only on x-raying. The criteria by which secondary bone tumours can be diagnosed is discussed later, suffice it to say here that it is generally not a difficult task, but one which in which radiography is often helpful. Malignant tumours occur rarely in skeletal assemblages and although this has sometimes been taken as evidence that cancer is a modern disease, the number of cases which is found is probably in line with expectation (see chapter 11 for further details).

Other forms of malignant disease which may affect the skeleton include leukaemia and multiple myelomatosis. Archaeological evidence for leukaemia is — so far as I am aware — virtually non-existent, but several cases of myeloma have been described. Myeloma is due to the proliferation of a particular type of bone marrow cell — the plasma cell — which secretes a factor which causes the increased resorption of bone by osteoclasts. The result is the production of holes in the skull, ribs, pelvis and other bones which mimic those produced by secondary tumour. It is often difficult to differentiate between the lesions of myeloma and secondary tumour with any confidence, but the abnormal plasma cells secrete a peculiar protein which can be extracted from the skeleton and used to verify a diagnosis.[1]

Death resulting from malignant diseases can be attributed to very few individuals but as seems so often to be the case, the skeletal evidence is deficient and we can be sure that many more people in the past died of cancer than is suggested by their remains. The reason for this is simply that even those tumours which have a propensity to spread to bone do not necessarily do so. At most, three quarters of breast and prostate tumours do, but not much more than a third of lung tumours spread to bone. Any estimates of the numbers dying from cancer in the past will be a serious underestimate, therefore, unless allowance is made for the 'non-appearance' of secondary spread.

Meningioma

Malignant tumours are those which spread from their site of origin. By contrast, benign tumours do not. One benign tumour, however, can nevertheless be fatal despite the fact that it remains *in situ* and this is the meningioma. Meningiomas are tumours which arise from the dura mater, the outermost covering of the brain. They may grow to a considerable size and in so doing raise the intra-cranial pressure with the ill effects on the brain stem mentioned above. Meningiomas may arise deep in the brain where they will produce no changes in the skull. Where they occur in the dura which is closely applied to the inner table of the skull, however, they may produce indentations which are mirror images of the original tumour. They can be recognised on the inner table of the skull,

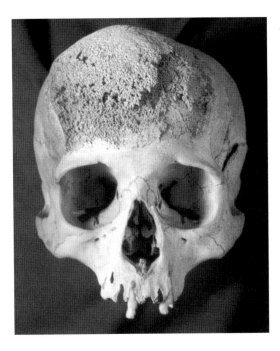

12 Skull showing extensive new bone on frontal bone caused by a meningionoma. Courtesy of San Diego Museum of Man

where they are accompanied by the impression of large blood vessels derived from the middle meningeal blood vessels. Those that have been described to date are usually small and would most likely have produced no symptoms. The frequency of meningiomas reported in human remains is very likely an underestimate as they cannot be seen if the skull is intact unless the interior is examined with an endoscope.[2] There is a more rare kind of meningioma which induces the formation of new bone which is visible on the external table of the skull. This is the variety which has most commonly been described since the changes are obvious in the intact skull.[3] Meningiomas of this type would have been invariably fatal, but again, death from this cause would have made an insignificant contribution to the overall death rate.

Infectious disease

When I started to become interested in palaeopathology I assumed that signs of infectious disease would be extremely common, and was surprised when this proved not to be the case. The most common human infections affect the soft tissues and do not generally involve the skeleton; a little thought might have spared my surprise! There are some exceptions, however: chronic varicose ulcers of the ankle may stimulate the underlying periosteum and lead to the production of an oval, raised area of new bone, usually on the tibia; some infections of the peripheral areas of the lung or of the overlying pleura may lead to new bone being laid down on the internal surface of the ribs; penetrating injuries to the bone or joints may cause localised osteomyelitis or to fusion of the joint. The nature of the infectious organism can usually only be guessed at, but in the future, the extraction of bacterial DNA with subsequent amplification and identification by the polymerase chain reaction should allow us be more definite on this point. Which, if any, of these non-specific infections caused or contributed towards death is completely unknown. There is a small number of specific infections, however, which we can be much more certain were implicated in the deaths those individuals in whose skeletons we find them to be present; these are osteomyelitis, tuberculosis, syphilis and, with some qualifications, leprosy.

Osteomyelitis

Osteomyelitis is an infection of the bone marrow and is most often caused by the spread of bacteria from elsewhere in the body via the blood stream. A common source of infection would have been boils or other skin infections caused by the *Staphylococcus aureus*. Osteomyelitis occurs most frequently in children and the bacteria in the bloodstream settle out at the growing ends of the long bones; the knee is an especially favoured site, but almost any bone can become infected. Having gained access to the bone marrow, the organisms multiply in what is an excellent culture medium and form pus which drains to the surface through channels called cloacae. The infection is chronic and was treatable only by amputation — a procedure which

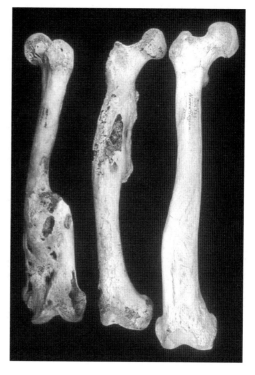

13 Three fractured femurs, two showing signs of osteomyelitis. Courtesy of San Diego Museum of Man

may have been more feared than the infection itself — until antibiotics became available. Individuals can live a long time with osteomyelitis but there are several serious complications which may prove fatal. The first is that the bacteria spread to other organs setting up further infection there; spread to the brain or to the spinal cord would quickly have been fatal. Similarly, death would quickly follow from septicaemia, that is, the condition in which the bacteria actually multiply in the blood as opposed to merely being transported by it (bacteraemia). An unusual complication of osteomyelitis is the production in the kidney of a complicated protein containing a compound called amyloid. This may develop to such an extent that the function of the kidney is seriously compromised, resulting in death from kidney failure. Whatever the ultimate cause of death of those in whom signs of osteomyelitis are found, it is reasonable to suppose the osteomyelitis was at the bottom of it.

Tuberculosis

Tuberculosis infections in man are primarily one of two kinds, those caused by the *Mycobacterium tuberculosis* or by *M. bovis*. The former is exclusive to humans while the latter has its normal home in cattle and other bovids. The human variety is spread by droplet infection through the air and the bovine form, through the agency of infected milk and other dairy products. The relationship between the two and their natural history in man is discussed later in the book.

Both forms of the disease may result in bone infections, usually of the spine, but almost any bone or joint may be involved. In the spine, infection causes a loss of bone substance with subsequent collapse of one or more vertebrae with the formation of a sharp angulation in the spine which is often referred to as Pott's disease. The human form of the disease, in which the lungs are affected, has a very high case fatality rate in the absence of modern antibiotic treatment and it was the pulmonary form of the disease which caused consumption, so common in nineteenth-century novels. The bovine form is a much more indolent disease in which the target organs are the lymph nodes and is only dangerous when complications set in. There is no way of telling from the morphological appearances of the changes in the skeleton which form of the disease is (or was) present.

Spinal collapse may itself have serious consequences, causing difficulties in breathing or neurological complications, but these would not necessarily be fatal. Spread of the organisms from the spine (or indeed elsewhere) is a much more likely precursor of death; spread to the brain or meninges being likely to cause death more quickly than any other complication.

As with osteomyelitis, it is safe to assume that the finding of tuberculosis in a skeleton is indicative that the individual died from the disease. It is possible, indeed probable, that some of the individuals in whom there are *no* changes consistent with tuberculosis were also infected and died as a result, and it is now possible to test this idea, as I will describe later.

Syphilis

Syphilis is one of a group of four human diseases caused by the family of treponemes, *Treponema pallidum* in the case of syphilis. As is well known, the disease is spread by sexual intercourse and passes through two brief stages which are self limiting and which raise false hopes in the infected individual, only to be dashed twenty or so years later when the symptoms of the tertiary stage make their appearance. The origins of the disease will be considered later, but syphilis has had its ups and downs, becoming common in the eighteenth century and almost banished in the twentieth with the advent of penicillin to which the organism is very sensitive; it is now experiencing something of a revival again and is increasing in frequency once more.

The tertiary stage of syphilis is marked by effects on the cardiovascular system, the nervous system and on the bone. The appearances in the bone were first described in detail by Cecil Hackett and still provide the basis for the diagnosis in the skeleton;[4] the skeletal effects are not fatal, however. The effects on the nervous system result in what used to be called general paralysis of the insane, précising the damage to both the brain and the peripheral nerves; that was fatal. So too were some of the effects on the cardiovascular system. Where the treponemes settled out in the walls of the large blood vessels, they set in train a series of events which weakened the vessel wall, causing the formation of a swelling or aneurysm. If the aneurysm burst, as it was prone to do, then death inevitably followed, and in pretty quick time. The descending aorta is the site which seems especially prone to syphilitic aneurysms, and the pulsation of the aneurysm against the body of the lumbar vertebrae would in time produce a pressure defect which can be recognised in the skeleton.

There was no effective treatment for syphilis until the eighteenth century when the use of mercury ointments was introduced. Treatment was prolonged and the saying at the time was that a night with Venus led to a lifetime with Mercury; not a very good exchange. Much of the early knowledge of the toxicity of mercury was gained from the treatment of syphilis; the physicians of the day would know that their patients were continuing with treatment when they began to show the symptoms of mercury poisoning. I am not sure how effective the treatment was, nor do I know of any research which has been carried out to try to find out. But, as with the other conditions I have mentioned so far, any skeleton that has the stigmata of syphilis is of an individual who died from it.

Leprosy

This disease is caused by infection with a mycobacterium (*M. leprae*) which is similar to that which causes tuberculosis. Leprosy takes a variety of forms in man, depending on the immunological response which is provoked by the infectious agent. Broadly speaking there are two forms, in one of which the nerves are damaged with subsequent sensory loss. The consequences of this sensory loss are that the joints of the leg may be subjected to unusual trauma resulting in misalignment and destruction; a similar change may be seen in tertiary syphilis and the affected joints are referred to as Charcot joints, after the nineteenth-century French neurologist who first described them. The second consequence of sensory loss in leprosy is that the foot becomes infected, especially if shoes are not worn, and osteomyelitis may supervene. There is then the potential for the complications described above. Very few skeletons have been described with leprosy in this country and there is no sure way of knowing how many of the individuals contracted the disease, nor in how many it contributed to their death.

I doubt if the cause of death could confidently be ascribed to more than a handful of skeletons in a large assemblage — certainly less than one in a hundred — due to the nigh impossibility of diagnosing fatal soft tissue diseases from skeletal remains. When death is caused intentionally, however, there is a better prospect of being able to come to a definitive diagnosis as I will try to show in the next chapter.

7 Death by intention

It is simply astonishing the time and effort which has been devoted to finding increasingly cruel ways of torturing, maiming and putting others to death; the human mind seems to be particularly inventive at finding new ways of inflicting pain and suffering. Nowhere is this better illustrated than in the various ways in which the law has decreed that those who have offended against it shall be tortured or executed. In this country, common criminals were generally executed by hanging, the nobility preferring to have their lives ended by beheading with the sword or the axe; the benefits which this supposedly conferred upon them are not immediately obvious, however. Some other forms of death by intention include suicide, ritual murder and killing for the pot, and these are the subject of the present chapter.

Suicide

Examples of suicide in archaeology are rare, for how can you know whether someone took their own life in the absence of a note, or in the absence of finding them buried at a crossroads with a stake through their heart, which was the prescribed fate of suicides until 1823? Depression is not a new disease and it is conceivable that some individuals in the past found life so intolerable that they could not continue with it and perhaps some of those who are found with severe injuries did jump; others may have opened veins or hanged themselves, but even where skeletal evidence exists, it is not evidence which can, in the main, point to suicide. There are — as always — exceptions.

William Leschallas died on 13 December 1852 and was buried in the crypt of Christ Church, Spitalfields five days later. His body was among those excavated between 1984 and 1986 and his coffin had a coffin plate still attached to it from which his name and dates of death and burial could be read. There were three holes in his skull: one, approximately 10.5 x 16mm, in the greater wing of the right sphenoid; a second (*c*.20 x 10mm) in the right parietal; and the third almost circular hole (*c*.28mm in diameter) just above the lambda at the back of the skull. At the time of the first examination, it was felt that the holes had been made post mortem, although not a great deal of thought was given to what event after death might have been responsible for them. An x-ray was performed on the skull and although some radio-opaque dots were seen on the film, it was considered to be unremarkable. Since Leschallas died after 1837, the year in which it became compulsory

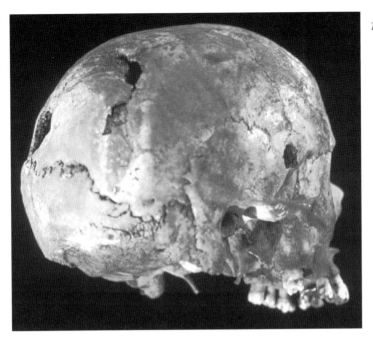

14 *Skull of male from Spitalfields with gunshot wounds. The entry wound is seen at the front of the skull and the larger exit wound at the back. (See text for further detail)*

to register deaths, a copy of his death certificate was obtained where the cause of death was given as: 'Shooting himself in the head with a pistol bullet died in a few minutes. Temporary insanity.'

This case was instructive in many ways. It certainly indicated to the BS who provided the first pathological report not to dismiss holes in the head so lightly, and I have never done so since. To dismiss things one cannot explain as being due to post mortem damage is unforgivable unless the nature of the post mortem damage can itself be explained. What had happened was that Leshallas had held the pistol to his head with his right hand, the bullet had gone forwards, bounced off the clivus and been deflected backward to exit through the back of his head. When the x-ray was examined more carefully, the radio-opaque dots were particles of lead around the entry wound and on the clivus. The first and third holes were caused by the entry and exit of the bullet; the third could not be explained and its cause is still a mystery.[1]

The inquest into Leschallas's death was reported in *The Times* on 14 December 1852. He had been a prosperous wholesale stationary manufacturer and exporter and rag merchant, the rags being the raw material for his paper making. The year before his death his paper mill in Chatham had burned down and he became convinced that he was on the verge of financial ruin, despite repeated reassurances to the contrary. The account of his mental state at the inquest leaves little doubt that he was depressed, and had probably been so for some time as he had attempted to take his life on an earlier occasion in March. The jury returned a verdict of temporary insanity which allowed the body to be interred in holy ground.

Leschallas's case is a good example of BS ignoring things they don't expect to find. Bullet wounds are rare or unknown in the periods from which the majority of human remains derive and are not an expected occurrence; all those involved in the case learnt that some of most interesting observations are those which are unexpected.

Shortly after the publication of Leschallas's case, a similar case was reported, this time from burials in the crypt of St Bride's in Fleet Street.[2] This was of a young man, Robert Edward R——, who died on 8 July 1821 at the age of 25. He too had taken his life with a pistol but had shot himself through the mouth. The entry wound was in the palate and the exit wound was in the left parietal bone close to the sagittal suture. The report of his death in the *Morning Chronicle* of 31 July 1821 noted that

> He had been subject for some time to rheumatism in the head, which caused excruciating pain. Verdict — mental derangement.

This verdict permitted this young man also to be buried in consecrated ground and it is possible that coroners were disposed to come to this verdict in order that this might happen in cases of suicide. If so, then it would have spared the relatives even more grief.

What the condition was from which Robert R suffered and that was so severe that only death could make it tolerable is uncertain, but it was definitely not one of the rheumatic diseases as we understand them nowadays. The most probable candidate is that he suffered from migraine, which can be excruciating and may occur in clusters. In the absence of any satisfactory painkillers, death might easily seem a preferable alternative to life with migraine.

Executions

The usual forms of execution in this country have been beheading and hanging. Beheading results in characteristic damage to the skeleton and there should be no difficulty in recognising it. Finding a body buried with its head between its knees will generally alert the excavator to the fact that something is not quite right and the BS should quickly be able to confirm the provisional diagnosis. It has been suggested, apparently quite seriously, that some individuals had their heads cut off after they were dead and this practice was the cause for their unusual appearances after death. There seems no way to confirm or refute this idea although common sense might suggest that this would be an unusual way to treat one's recently departed relatives, and what benefit such a procedure would confer on either the living or dead parties is hard to imagine. We will continue to assume that most skeletons with evidence of beheading suffered at the hands of the law rather than their next of kin.

Beheading

The evidence for decapitation comes from finding that one of the cervical vertebrae has been transected, sometimes with additional damage to the back of the mandible, the mastoid processes or the first rib. A study of a large number of decapitated burials suggests that the blow was usually struck from back to front and that the cut passed through the upper cervical vertebrae, although sometimes the seventh cervical or even the first thoracic were involved.[3]

On one occasion I found it possible to identify an individual by the fact that he had been beheaded. Simon Burley was adviser and tutor to Richard II but sentenced to death by what is known as the Merciless Parliament during which five of Richard's favourites were accused of treason. Queen Anne begged for Burley's life on her knees, but despite her intervention he was executed at Tower Hill on 5 May 1388, having the unwelcome distinction of being the first person executed on that spot. He was buried in the church of St Mary Graces in London which had been built on the site of a Black Death cemetery. During excavations of the church a poorly preserved skeleton was found among the other bodies recovered from the site. Amongst the rather small collection of bones present were some cervical vertebrae with clear evidence of decapitation on the fourth. The cut had sliced through the superior surface and through the facet joints and it seemed clear that this was all that was left of Simon Burley.

Hanging

Hanging seems to have been introduced into Britain by the Anglo-Saxons and it became the method used most frequently to execute those sentenced to death. Until the nineteenth century hanging was conducted with a running noose which was hung from a rudimentary gallows of some other handy structure like the branch of a tree. The victim was either hoisted up by the rope which was then tied, leaving him dangling in place, or he might be placed on a cart with the noose about his neck, the cart withdrawn to leave him suspended until he strangled to death. During the later Medieval period, and well into the eighteenth century, the condemned man climbed a ladder with the noose about his neck, the executioner fastened the rope to the cross beam of the gallows and then 'turned off' the victim; sometimes friends of the condemned man would pull on his legs to try to hasten his death. Hanging was never intended to be a quick or a merciful death, but it was meant to be an exemplary punishment, the horrific nature of the death serving as a deterrent to those who might otherwise be tempted to transgress. The degree to which the condemned man suffered during his execution is not — cannot be — known, but there are scores of accounts of public executions where the victims were seen to struggle for many minutes. There are a few accounts from the eighteenth century of individuals who survived hanging, but their recollection of the event is not surprisingly vague, and no doubt clouded by the overwhelming joy at still being alive.

Hanging with a running noose results in death from cerebral anoxia brought about by compression of the carotid arteries which can occur with the application of surprisingly little force, inhibition of the vagal nerve, and closure of the airway. It is possible that unconsciousness came about quite quickly, although those who state this with some confidence lack any first-hand evidence to confirm it, and the pulse may continue to beat for many minutes. The struggles so commonly observed by onlookers at hangings may have been nothing more than reflex jerking of the muscles brought about by lack of oxygen. Executions were frequently bungled because the executioner was incompetent, drunk, or both, and during the nineteenth century the drop was introduced in the attempt to make the procedure more humane and more efficient. Up to this point, the knot had always been placed at the back of the neck, but with the drop, the knot was placed beneath the ear, usually on the left side. In some countries the knot was placed under the chin as it was said this caused instantaneous death as the spinal cord was crushed by the dislocated cervical vertebrae; this placement of the knot was never introduced in this country.

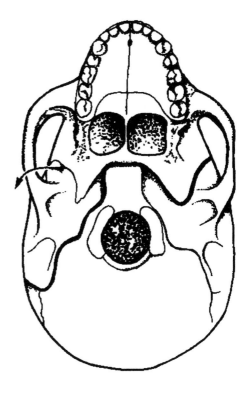

Skeletal lesions caused by hanging

There has been much debate and discussion about the skeletal lesions that follow hanging. One of the earliest descriptions was given by Frederic Wood Jones who reported finding the skeletons

15 Base of skull showing disruption of sutures consequent upon hanging. Arrow shows side on which the know was presumed to have been placed. After Wood Jones

of 100 Nubian men who had been executed by the Romans. The skeletons were in two trenches, some with the rope still around their neck. Wood Jones found that in some of the skeletons the sutures at the base of the skull had been pulled open on the side on which the knot (presumably) had been placed (**15**).[4] Wood Jones continued his research into the subject when he returned from Egypt, experimenting by dropping cadavers down the lift shaft of the anatomy school at St Thomas's Hospital in which dubious practice he was assisted by his head of department. He also examined the remains of five men who had been hanged in Rangoon Central Jail with a knot under the chin and found that there was a fracture dislocation through the posterior arch of the axis, the body of which remained attached to the third cervical vertebra. This fracture came to be known at the hangman's fracture, now frequently seen in those injured in traffic accidents (**16**).

Later studies on the remains of executed criminals in South Africa showed that the axis had dislocated through the neural arch and that sometimes, the tip of the foramen transversarium had also been fractured.[5] In the largest study of the lesions caused by

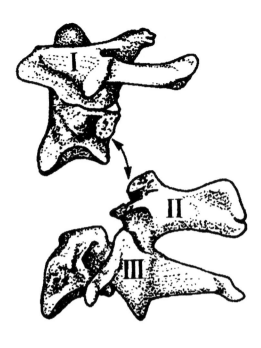

16 Diagram of hangman's fracture. The body of the axis and the odontoid peg remain fixed to the axis and the block is dislocated forward and upwards in the direction of arrow, to crush the cervical cord. After Wood Jones

hanging, the skeletons of 34 convicted murderers who had been hanged at three prisons in Britain between 1882 and 1945 were examined. There were no fractures at the base of the skull and in only seven cases had the cervical vertebrae been fractured, one of those through a congenitally abnormal third cervical. The other six fractures of the cervical vertebrae were through the axis and were of two types, one conforming to the hangman's fracture and a second type in which the axis was fractured through the neural arch on the right side, parallel to the odontoid peg (**17**).[6]

The possibility exists, therefore, that the skeletons of executed criminals will show fractures of the neck which will point to their cause of death, at least after the introduction of the drop, but to the best of my knowledge, none has yet been found. I have found a single skull belonging to a young woman who was buried in the cemetery of St Brides Lower Churchyard in London with a disruption of the sutures of the base of the skull, similar to that described by Wood Jones. The cemetery had been used in the early nineteenth century and there is an entry in the parish records which refers to a young woman and her brother who were hanged before being buried there. It is tempting to suppose that the skull was that of this young woman.

Hanging with a running noose is not likely to leave any signs on the skeleton but some features of the burial may suggest that death was due to hanging. Some bodies, for example, appear to have had their hands tied behind their backs or in front of them and if they have not been decapitated — as is sometimes the case — then it is inferred that they have been hanged. Prone burials are sometimes also interpreted as being those of executed criminals.

The examination of two skeletons which were removed *en bloc* from Galley Hill in Surrey showed that both had had their hands tied behind their backs, and in one of the skeletons the fingers were flexed at the inter-phalangeal joints, much as one might expect in someone under great stress or in great pain (**18**). There was no damage to the skull or the neck, but there seemed enough circumstantial evidence to suppose that both men had been hanged.

Bog bodies

In August 1984, the peat cutters working in Lindow Moss in Cheshire were surprised to find a human foot in what they thought was a piece of wood among the peat they were feeding through the mill. The police were called, followed by the county archaeologist who was able to locate the rest of the body of an individual who was informally known as Pete Marsh, later as Lindow Man.[7] Radiocarbon dating suggested that the body dated to the late Iron Age or to the Roman period and the body was of a powerfully built young man of about 25 years of age and 1.68m in height. He had a thong around the neck which was thought to be a garrotte, his throat appeared to have

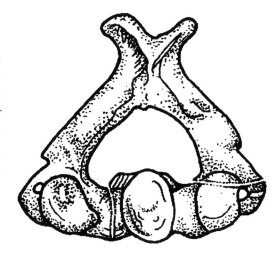

17 *Alternate type of fracture caused by hanging. The fracture lines on the axis run in the transverse direction (on the right side of the diagram) and from front to back (on the left side). After James and Nasmyth-Jones*

been cut on the right side, there were lacerations on the head, and his neck had been dislocated. Lindow Man had clearly been killed as some part of a ritual sacrifice and then his body disposed of in the bog.

Well over 100 bog bodies have been found in the British Isles and there are several more known on the Continent, some of which have almost achieved celebrity status

18 *Left hand of an Anglo-Saxon male in situ. The fingers — especially that of the third and fourth fingers — can be seen tightly flexed at the proximal inter-phalangeal joints. This individual was assumed to have been hanged*

through the publication of P.V. Glob's book, *The Bog People* in which he suggested that his Iron Age victims had been sacrificed to a goddess of fertility.[8] Wherever they are found, bog bodies attract immense public interest, and as with the Ice Man, they serve as a magnet for all manner of BS who hie off in the hope of getting their hands, if not on the body itself, then at least on a bit of it. The bodies provide information on some aspects of ritual in the past, but rather little about anything else, and the artefacts found with them are often more interesting than the bodies themselves. Bog bodies are seldom more revealing about disease in the past than the skeleton although they do have the potential for yielding evidence of soft tissue lesions. Since they provide no more than a sample of one, what findings *may* come to light cannot be generalised to a larger population, so their epidemiological value is also small. They do serve the useful purpose of keeping the study of human remains in the public eye, however, and to deprecate their examination as no more than glory archaeology is to rather overstate the case.

Bog bodies have come to light in earlier periods than ours, and the fens of Cambridge and Norfolk have been particularly fruitful in this respect, and it is possible that it was a bog body that gave rise to the legend of the incorruptibility of the body of St Edmund. Edmund was king of East Anglia and was killed in battle with the Danes in *c*.870. The legend of his death states that he was martyred by being tied to a tree and shot at with arrows, and then beheaded. The Danes left the body where it was but threw the head into a bramble bush from where it called out to those who came to look for Edmund and take him for burial. The body was originally buried in a makeshift chapel later to be transferred to a church at Boedericsworth and, via a spell in London, laid finally to rest in Bury St Edmunds. Edmund's tomb was opened two or three times in the Middle Ages when the body — with the head attached — was found to be incorrupt. The body was stolen from Bury by the French in 1217 and allegedly taken to Toulouse to the church of St Sernin. The remains which are said to be the relics of St Edmund are most certainly not those of an incorruptible body, and the true fate of the body buried at Bury St Edmunds will never be known. The legend of the incorruptible body may well have arisen, however, from the original finding of a bog body which would be preserved for a long time without further attention.

Cannibalism

There are few more emotive subjects than cannibalism, and although I have not seen BS actually come to blows when discussing it, they do become more heated than about any other topic in their field. Ethnologists have recorded dozens of examples of cannibalism but they are all based on hearsay evidence. No one seems to have ever witnessed anyone eating human flesh, and Williams Arens concluded that cannibalism was a myth; he could find no instance where the practice had been observed, and where it was reported it was always others who were said to indulge, never the reporters.[9]

No one disputes that ritual cannibalism has taken place, or that humans have been eaten by survivors of accidents or shipwrecks, or during periods of intense starvation; the arguments hinge around whether humans were ever used routinely as a source of protein. Evidence that cannibalism was a common practice has been presented most recently by Tim White and Christie and Jacqueline Turner based on their examination of remains from Anasazi sites in the American south-west. The key to their interpretation is the similarity between the cut marks and butchery marks found on human and animal bones from the same sites, often co-mingled suggesting that all the bones are kitchen waste. White noted that both human and animal bones showed modifications which were consistent with defleshing, disarticulation, breakage and cooking.[10] White's book was greeted with dismay by anthropologists, archaeologists and representatives of the native American tribes alike and his interpretation was not widely accepted. The Turners examined evidence from all the sites in the American Southwest where cannibalism or inter-personal violence had been claimed.[11] It has been suggested that the 'minimal taphonomic signature' of cannibalism would require six criteria:

- breakage of bones to get at the brain or bone marrow

- cut marks suggestive of butchery

- anvil abrasions where the bone has rested on a stone anvil while being broken

- absence of vertebrae (which were assumed to be boiled or crushed to get out the bone marrow or grease)

- burning

- pot polishing on the ends of bones which were supposed to have cooked and stirred in clay pots

Of the 76 sites which they investigated, the Turners concluded that 38 were identifiable as cannibalism and 19 as cases of interpersonal violence. They estimated that at least 286 men, women and children had been consumed at the cannibal sites and that the victims had generally been beaten before being put to death. There is no doubt that the human bones from these sites have many of the characteristics which are taken to indicate butchery in animal bones, but the matter is still fiercely debated and alternative explanations are being put forward. One interesting hypothesis is that the bones are those of witches and their families who were put to death and their bodies cut up or burnt to prevent the witch from reinhabiting his or her body.[12] Unless and until a group of people is actually caught with a human joint in the pot, the arguments will continue, neither side yielding to the other in their convictions.

Part 3: Disease

8 Aching joints

Most diseases which afflict us arise in the soft tissues, but only those which secondarily involve the skeleton can be diagnosed in bare bones. These, and the diseases which arise directly in the bone, account for only a fraction of the total of all disease, thus the BS's description of disease in the past is necessarily fragmentary and incomplete.

Bone is a complex structure being composed of collagen fibres between which is laid down the hard crystalline matrix which is known as hydroxy-apatite, composed principally of hydrated calcium phosphate. During life the crystalline part of the bone is being continually turned over to provide calcium for vital functions. Two kinds of cells are involved in this process, the osteoblasts which lay down bone, and the osteoclasts which resorb it. There is a constant cycle of osteoblast and osteoclast activity and the skeleton is renewed approximately every ten years so that a seventy year old will have had six or seven new skeletons during his lifetime. In the mature skeleton the activity of the osteoclasts and the osteoblasts is synchronised and the bones retain their normal shape, and the mass of the skeleton remains constant until late middle age when it starts to decline. Skeletal mass falls most quickly in post-menopausal women and may lead to osteoporosis with potentially serious consequences, most notably fractures of the vertebrae, femoral neck and forearm.

Pathological events in the skeleton are an exaggeration of those which occur naturally, that is to say, they result in the acquisition of new bone or the loss of bone, and sometimes both. Pathological new bone does not obey the normal rules, and is generally not remodelled and diseased bones are frequently recognised by their abnormal appearance, either by direct examination or on an x-ray. Similarly, where bone is lost as the result of a disease, it is not replaced, or replaced inadequately.

Joint disease

Joint disease is by far the most common pathological change found in the skeleton and usually accounts for at least a third of all the pathology in a skeletal assemblage. Dozens of different joint diseases have been described, most rare and unusual, and the BS need concern himself with only a few, including osteoarthritis, rheumatoid arthritis, ankylosing spondylitis, gout and DISH. Osteoarthritis and DISH are characterised by bone formation, whereas in the others, bone loss is the most important feature and they are sometimes collectively known as erosive arthropathies (erosions being the areas of bone loss).

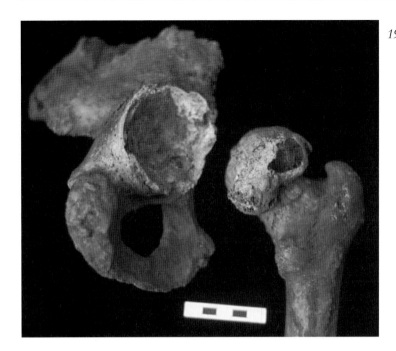

19 Osteoarthritis of the hip showing considerable development of marginal osteophyte. The eburnation which was present on both joint surfaces does not show up in the photograph

Osteoarthritis

Osteoarthritis is a disease of very great antiquity having been found throughout all periods of the archaeological record. Osteoarthritis (OA) is common at the present day and it has been estimated that about 8 million in the UK have OA, but only about 1 million seek medical help because the affected joints are painful. The rest of the population with OA may be completely unaware that their joints are 'diseased' and they may become aware of it only as an incidental finding when they have an x-ray, for example. It is important to remember that osteoarthritic joints are not necessarily painful when interpreting changes found in past populations.

There are different kinds of joint in the body, but the most common by far is known as a synovial joint, and it is this type of joint which is affected by OA. In the normal synovial joint, the ends of the bones are covered with a layer of cartilage which acts as a shock absorber within the joint. The joint is surrounded by a thin membrane — the synovial membrane — which secretes fluid into the joint. This synovial fluid acts both to lubricate the joint and to supply nourishment to the articular cartilage; under normal conditions the joint surfaces are virtually frictionless. The joint is held firmly in place by ligaments which attach to the articulating bones, and the whole is surrounded by a fibrous joint capsule. The tendons of the muscles which act on the joint are attached to the bones at points which are known as entheses (**20**).

In OA, the articular cartilage thins and new bone is laid down around the margin of the joint; this new bone is known as osteophyte. As the disease progresses, more and more cartilage is lost, the amount of osteophyte increases and the shape of the articulating ends of the bone changes. Eventually, all the cartilage may be lost and the bare bone ends come

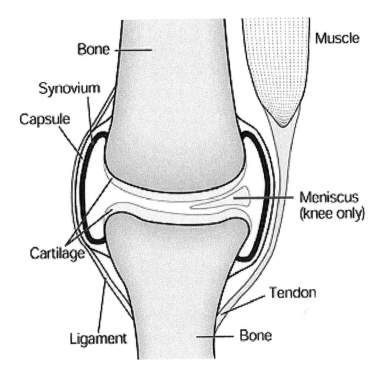

20 Diagram of
   normal synovial
   joint

Bone

Muscle

Synovium

Capsule

Meniscus
(knee only)

Cartilage

Tendon

Ligament

Bone

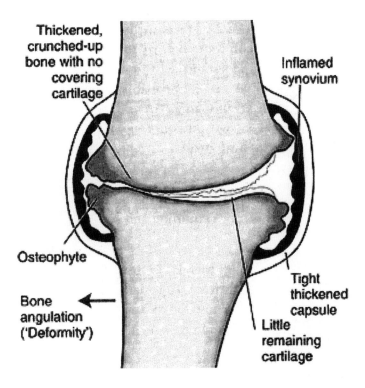

21 Diagram of
   synovial joint
   affected by
   osteoarthritis

Thickened,
crunched-up
bone with no
covering
cartilage

Inflamed
synovium

Osteophyte

Bone
angulation
('Deformity')

Tight
thickened
capsule

Little
remaining
cartilage

into contact with each other and rub together to produce a hard shiny area on their surface which is referred to as eburnation (**21**). New bone may form on the joint surfaces and they may also become pitted. In some cases, there may be so much osteophyte formed around the reciprocal margins of the joint that the range of movement is limited or even prevented.

It was formerly thought that OA was the result of degeneration of the joint which was especially likely to occur with advancing age, but it is now known that the changes represent the efforts of the joint to repair itself. In some cases, especially in the small joints of the fingers, repair may be successful, but this is seldom true of the large joints. In modern clinical practice, the most common sites found to be affected are the knee, hip, hand, big toe and neck. This is because when these joints become arthritic they tend to be painful, and it is pain which takes the patient to seek medical aid. We will see later that the pattern of involvement is different in skeletal assemblages.

Osteoarthritis is caused by the interaction of various precipitating factors in conjunction with an hereditary predisposition, and as we have seen earlier (chapter 3) there is no way in which one can determine which factor or factors were involved in a particular case. The diagnosis of OA in the skeleton differs from either the clinical or radiological diagnosis made in the clinic. The clinical diagnosis is made largely on the basis of pain, together with finding a number of signs in the affected joint, including swelling and crepitus, a grinding sensation which can be felt when the joint moves. Radiologically, the diagnosis depends on finding narrowing of the joint space and the presence of marginal osteophyte. The articular cartilage separates the ends of the bones but because it is not opaque to x-rays, there appears to be a space between the bones on a radiograph. In a joint affected by OA, the cartilage thins and the joint space narrows. The BS is in no position to know whether or not his subjects were in pain; they certainly cannot tell him so, and, of course, since the bones are disarticulated, no estimate of joint space narrowing can be made. The diagnosis of OA in the skeleton therefore has to be based on other criteria. Finding eburnation in a joint is a sure sign that the articular cartilage has disappeared and that the two ends of the articulating bones were in contact; in other words it is a pathognomonic sign of OA. The safest way of diagnosing OA in the skeleton is to rely on finding eburnation, but if eburnation is *not* present, we have suggested that it can be diagnosed when at least *two* of the following signs are present:[1]

- marginal osteophyte and/or new bone on the joint surface

- pitting on the joint surface

- alteration in the bony contour of the joint

In practice there is much to be lost by ignoring these minor signs and basing the diagnosis solely on the basis of finding eburnation. In this way, we would at least know that like is being compared with like in comparative studies.

The characteristics of OA in past populations

The prevalence of OA in past populations seems to be lower than at the present but this is almost certainly an artefact caused by the non-random nature of the skeletal samples and by differences in diagnosis. It does conform to modern experience in some important ways, however; it is increasingly common with increasing age, and tends to be slightly more common in women than in men. The distribution of OA in the past is different, however, and there have been some changes over time. In all skeletal assemblages, the most commonly affected joints are the facet joints of the spine and the acromio-clavicular joint of the shoulder; OA of the hands is common, but OA of the hip and knee is much less frequent, a notable difference between

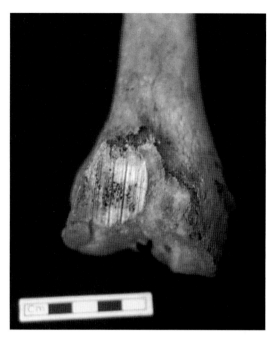

22 *Osteoarthritis of the patello-femoral joint. The eburnation on the femur is clearly visible and there is pitting and grooving on the joint surface*

palaeopathological and clinical experience. Two interesting changes seem to have occurred in the post-medieval period. The first concerns OA of the large joints. In the medieval period, OA of the hip was more common than OA of the knee, whereas the converse is true in the post-medieval period, and this confirms with clinical experience. The knee is a complex joint, having three compartments, one between the patella and the femur and two (medial and lateral) between the femur and tibia. Patients with painful knee OA seem to have involvement of the medial tibio-femoral compartment and skeletal studies suggest that this form of the disease is of very recent origin, perhaps arising only in the last two hundred years or so.[2] The second change relates to the pattern of OA in the hands. During the medieval period disease affecting only one joint (or one set of joints) was most common, whereas in the post-medieval period, multi-focal disease became more common.[3] Interestingly, there is a strong relationship between OA of the knee and hand in skeletons from eighteenth- and ninteenth-contexts in London, which is found in modern populations.[4]

To explain these changes in the patterns of OA we must refer again to the model (*see* **3**) and there are not many options to consider. There can have been no change in genetic disposition as the time is far too short for this to have happened. The most likely candidates are changes in activity or in weight — and by inference, in nutrition. Of the two, I would plump for changes in weight, consequent upon dietary changes. It is surely no coincidence that that the two sites concerned are those which are most strongly related to obesity. A study of weight and/or physique in skeletons with and without OA of the knee or hand in both periods might shed some further light on these changes.

The erosive arthropathies

The erosive arthropathies are characterised by discrete areas of bone loss — so-called erosions — in the joint. The classic erosive joint disease is rheumatoid arthritis which affects about 1% of the adult population. Women are more likely to be affected than men, in a ratio of about 3:1 and the peak incidence is in the 30s. Rheumatoid arthritis (RA) is a disease of the synovial membrane which becomes infiltrated with inflammatory cells which causes it to become thickened and vascular. The diseased synovial membrane is referred to as a pannus, and as the disease progresses it grows from the joint margin to cover and then destroy the articular cartilage. As these changes take place, erosions form, first around the margins of the joint and then on the joint surfaces. In advanced cases, the joints become deformed and may dislocate but it is rare for joints other than those of the wrist or the foot to fuse. The end stage of the disease is a crippling deformity of the hands and other joints and it hard to believe that the extremes of the disease would have been missed by writers or artists in former times had the disease been as common as it is now.

Rheumatoid arthritis characteristically affects the small joints of the hands and feet, especially the proximal inter-phalangeal joints and the metacarpo-phalangeal and metatarso-phalangeal joints. The changes are almost always symmetrical and the sacro-iliac joints are almost never involved; an important feature in differentiating RA from other erosive joint disease. Almost any other joint may be affected as the disease progresses but most commonly the wrist, knee, cervical spine, shoulder, sub-talar joint, elbow and hip. In RA new bone formation is minimal and the bones around affected joints are often osteoporotic.

About three-quarters of modern patients with RA have antibodies (usually IgM antibodies) to IgG molecules in their blood and this antibody is referred to as rheumatoid factor. In theory it should be possible to extract rheumatoid factor from bones, but the few instances in which this has been tried have not proved successful.

The diagnosis of RA in human remains depends upon finding a symmetrical erosive arthropathy affecting the small joints of the hands and the feet, with minimal new bone formation. Where the joints have been badly damaged and the cartilage destroyed, there may be eburnation on the joint surfaces but the other changes present allow this easily to be differentiated from primary OA. Difficulties in diagnosis arise because the bones are fragile, due to being osteoporotic, and may be damaged after death or during excavation, and important elements may be missing. I do not think that the diagnosis can ever be made with confidence if the hands and feet are missing, and never on the basis of changes in a single large joint such as the elbow or shoulder. This will undoubtedly mean that the prevalence of RA in the past will be underestimated but this benefit will be — one hopes — in some conformity of diagnosis.

23 *Foot bones from a*
medieval female
skeleton showing
erosions on the
metatarsal heads in
rheumatoid arthritis

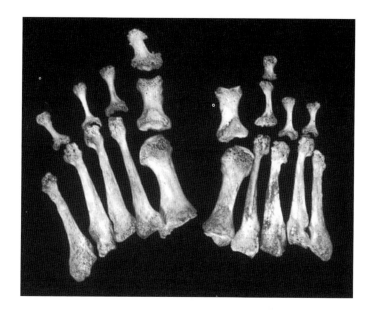

The erosions seen in RA are true erosions and should be distinguished from other holes, some of which are the points of entry of small blood vessels around the joint, which are frequently seen, especially in the wrist, ankle and around the shoulder. Radiography is sometimes helpful in distinguishing true from pseudo-erosions, showing the loss of bony cortex and trabeculae ending in mid-air; the erosions often have a dense white margin which the radiologists refer to as sclerosis and which indicates an attempt at repair. The erosions in RA always begin at the joint margin and encroach onto the joint surface as the disease progresses. A skeleton which is found with erosions on the joint surface but not at the margins has some form of erosive joint disease but not RA.

The clinical features of RA were first described in 1800 by Landré-Beauvais who believed that it was a variant of gout and called it *goutte astháenique primitive*. On this account it has sometimes been considered that RA is a new disease but skeletons with classic features of the disease have been described from the medieval period, in Europe and elsewhere[5] and it has been suggested that Rubens had progressive RA during the last 30 years of his life.[6] There is little doubt that RA is not a new disease, but its incidence may have changed in the eighteenth century so that it became more common and was brought to the attention of the physicians. It is interesting that the incidence of RA seems to be declining in the United States and Western Europe but is increasing in Africa as the result of life-style or environmental changes.[7]

The sero-negative arthropathies

In the 1960s it was found that some patients with what appeared to be a variant of rheumatoid arthritis did not have rheumatoid factor in their blood, and hence this group of joint disease came to be known as the sero-negative arthropathies (SNA). They comprise a group of erosive, inflammatory polyarthropathies in which the spine, the

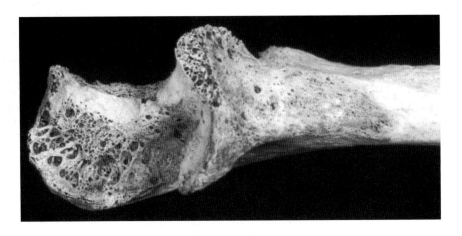

24 Proximal ulna from a medieval skeleton with rheumatoid arthritis. Virtually the whole of the normal joint surface has been destroyed and there are many erosions affecting the joint

sacro-iliac joints and the entheses are affected. Sacro-iliac involvement is an important point of differentiation between the sero-negative diseases and RA, especially in the skeleton.

The SNAs which may be found in the skeleton include Reiter's disease, psoriatic arthropathy and ankylosing spondylitis. Reiter's disease and psoriatic arthropathy (PA) share a number of clinical and radiological features in common although they can readily be distinguished clinically. As with RA, pathological changes start in the synovial membrane which becomes infiltrated with inflammatory cells, thickened and proliferative. The articular cartilage is destroyed as in RA, but in the SNAs there is a greater propensity for the joints to fuse. Marginal and central erosions may be seen and there is a good deal of new bone formation, unlike the situation in RA.

The other characteristic of the SNAs is the involvement of tendons, ligaments and entheses which may become ossified. The ossification of spinal ligaments accounts for the fusion of vertebrae which is almost always a feature of these conditions. New bone may occur on the bone shafts, particularly on the metatarsals in Reiter's disease.

Psoriatic arthropathy (PA) occurs in a small number of patients with psoriasis, a skin disease which affects about 1% of the population. The changes are asymmetrical and noted most often in the joints of the hand. The disease is usually mild but there is a severe, mutilating form in which the inter-phalangeal joints are destroyed with fusion and shortening of the fingers. The end result may clinically mimic those of RA and the changes may be confused with those caused by leprosy. In addition to sacro-iliac involvement, changes may be seen in the cervical spine.

Reiter's syndrome: Hans Reiter described the disease which came to bear his name in 1916 in a cavalry officer who had gonorrhoea. Nowadays the disease often arises in those with chronic gastro-intestinal disease and it is often referred to as reactive arthropathy rather than Reiter's disease. Males are more often affected than females and the peak incidence is between the ages of 15 and 35 years.

The changes in Reiter's disease are similar to those in PA; the erosions are asymmetrically distributed but are much more likely to be found in the feet than the hands. As well as the sacro-iliac changes, some of the vertebrae may be fused. The areas of fusion are interspersed between normal vertebrae and are referred to as 'skip' lesions. The entheses around the calcaneum are often ossified and there may be fluffy new bone on the metatarsal shafts, on the tibia or on the metacarpal shafts.

Ankylosing spondylitis (AS) is the most likely of the sero-negative arthropathies to be encountered in the skeleton, or in the palaeopathological literature. While many of the cases in the literature are undoubtedly genuine cases, others are not recognisable as what we now call AS. The confusion arises because many medical writers in the past used the term for *any* condition in which the vertebrae were fused. In the older literature, and still in some continental literature, the disease is

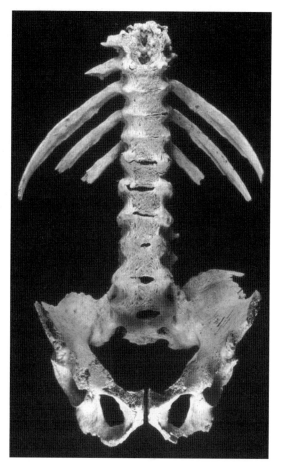

25 Spinal column and pelvis from skeleton with ankylosing spondylitis. The sacroiliac and all the vertebrae are fused; there are no skip lesions and some of the ribs are fused with the vertebrae.
Courtesy of San Diego Museum of Man

referred to as von Bechterew's disease or Marie-Strümpell disease; there is nothing to recommend the continued use of these terms, however.

The disease usually begins in the sacro-iliac joints and the lumbar spine. The sacro-iliac changes are symmetrical and both joints may fuse. In the spine the changes are noticed first at the insertion of the outer fibres of the inter-vertebral disc into the vertebral body and erosions may be seen in this position. The ligaments become ossified and as other ligaments become affected, the fusion spreads upwards until the spine may become completely fused and rigid, usually with some kyphosis. There are no skip lesions in AS, which helps differentiate it from reactive arthropathy. If the ligaments around the joints joining the ribs to the vertebrae become involved, the ribs fuse to the spine so that the pelvis, vertebral column and thoracic cage can be lifted as a single entity.

There is an important genetic component in AS and patients with the disease almost all have a tissue antigen referred to as HLA-B27 compared with 10% of the general population. The prevalence of AS shows great geographical variation; it is very rare in Japan, for example, and this reflects the low prevalence of HLA-B27. It is possible that the antigen could be extracted from human bone, but to the best of my knowledge this has not yet been attempted.

DISH

DISH — diffuse idiopathic skeletal hyperostosis — is condition characterised by exuberant new bone formation in the spinal and ossification of extra-spinal entheses. The changes in the spine result from ossification of the anterior longitudinal ligament (ALL), and although the entire length of the spinal column may be involved they are usually most prominent in the thoracic region. The formation of new bone has been likened to melting wax flowing down the spine and it produces a spectacular appearance in the skeleton. In time, ossification of the ALL leads to fusion of a variable number of vertebrae. The facet joints and the inter-vertebral disc spaces remain normal, however, so long as some other pathological process does not supervene.

A characteristic feature of DISH is that the changes in the thoracic region are confined to the right-hand side. It is thought that this is because the descending aorta lies over the left-hand side of the thoracic vertebrae and the pulsation of this large blood vessel prevents

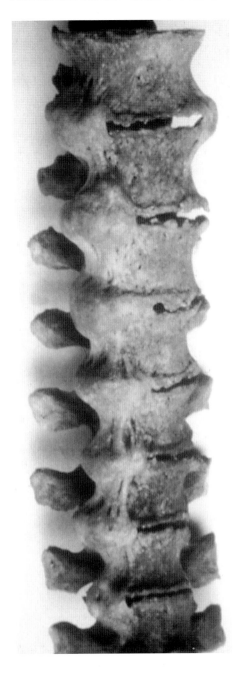

26 *Spinal column from a male skeleton with DISH. The flowing, right-sided new bone formation is clearly seen on the right-hand side of the thoracic vertebrae*

ossification of the ALL. Although this seems rather a lame explanation, the presence of the aorta has *something* to do with it, for in the rare condition in which the descending aorta overlies the *right* side of the thoracic vertebra, the changes of DISH are on the *left*.

Any of the extra-spinal entheses or ligaments may be affected but the most commonly involved are those of the pelvis, leading to sacro-iliac fusion, those around the calcaneum and patella, and the insertion of the triceps muscle into the olecranon process of the elbow.

DISH is given a lot of attention by BS because the changes are unmistakeable and there is usually no problem with diagnosis. Occasionally the tyro is persuaded to report dire consequences of the condition, but in fact most patients are unaware that they have it, or at most complain of some back stiffness or peripheral pain; back pain is not a feature of the condition. In rare cases, the posterior longitudinal ligament (PLL) is ossified and when this happens there is a danger that the spinal cord may be compressed with serious neurological changes.[8]

The cause of DISH is not known with any certainty. Its prevalence is highly age related and it rarely appears before the age of 40. In modern populations it has been associated with obesity and late onset (type II) diabetes. The crude prevalence in the over 40s is *c*.4% in men and 2.5% in women. It is more common in blacks than whites and the prevalence is low in Asians and Native Americans which suggests that some genetic factors may be involved.

In the archaeological context there seems to be a relationship between DISH and the monastic way of life. I came across this connection when I was examining some skeletons from the site of Merton Priory in which the prevalence of DISH was very much higher than expected and I reported this finding in the Christmas issue of the *British Medical Journal*, suggesting that it might be a 'new' occupational disease.[9] The Christmas issue is reserved for light-hearted papers and other trivia which do not require attention to be deflected from the nuts and Madeira, but nevertheless the relationship received confirmation from other BS and we were also able to show that the relationship held at other sites. For example, the prevalence of DISH in skeletons recovered from the church and chapels of Wells Cathedral and the abbey of St Mary Graces where the monks and lay benefactors would have been buried was considerably higher than in the skeletons recovered from the lay cemeteries, and statistical analysis of the results shows that the observed differences were scarcely likely to have arisen by chance (**Table 11**).[10]

The association between DISH and the monastic life is now well established and the cause is probably related to the monks' diet. When they were first established, the monastic orders lived under an austere regime taking one meal a day in winter and two from Easter to mid-September. There was a general prohibition against eating meat but ways were found to get round this restriction. In one thirteenth-century monastery in France, for example, the monks were permitted only to eat game which had been hunted whereupon they smuggled dogs into the monastery and persuaded them to chase pigs around the cloisters thus turning pork into game. Monks in the infirmary were also allowed to eat meat and so they entered the infirmary in turn in order to supplement their rations. In time the

Table 11 Prevalence of DISH in male burials from Wells Cathedral and the church of St Mary Graces, London

Site	Place of burial	No. of males	No. with DISH	Prevalence (%)
	Lay cemetry	93	6	6.5
Wells Cathedral	Lady chapel	15	2	13.3
	Stillington's chapel	13	3	23.1
St Mary Graces	Lay cemetery	99	0	–
	Church and chapels	52	6	11.5

dietary restrictions were relaxed and Barbara Harvey found from her examination of the kitchen rolls of Westminster Abbey that on an average day outside Advent and Lent, the monks had an allowance of 6,207 calories; during Advent the daily allowance was 5,291 but a measly 4,870 calories in Lent.[11] Of course the monks did not consume their entire daily ration — some was for the poor at the gate — but there is no doubt that the diet in a medieval monastery was rich and varied. Fish was always abundant, and there were quantities of game: capons, ducks, geese, egret, herons, pheasants, partridge, pigeons, quail, teal and swan are all mentioned in the account books of the fourteenth-century abbot of Westminster. In 1372 this same abbot gave a dinner at which beef, mutton, four small pigs, five ducks, one swan, six geese, six capon, nine fowl, two woodcock and a milk cream cheese were served, all washed down with a plentiful supply of wine or ale.

Small wonder, then, that DISH was common, especially when one realises that the daily calorie requirement for men with sedentary occupations is *c*.3,000 while the average lumberjack can get by on 4,500 calories a day. One cannot imagine that praying and contemplation used more energy than chopping down trees, and the spare calories must soon have been evident as growing waist lines — and the development of DISH.

Gout

Gout has been present to trouble man for thousands of years and a description can be found in the writings of Hippocrates. Thomas Sydenham, who himself suffered from the disease, wrote in the seventeenth century that the pain was 'like the bite of a dog'. The disease is caused by an inflammatory reaction to the deposition of uric acid crystals within the soft tissues around a joint. Gouty arthritis can be present in either an acute or a chronic form. The first attack of acute gout usually occurs in middle-aged men or in post-menopausal women. The affected joint rapidly becomes red and swollen and is exquisitely painful. The attacks are self-limiting and in between times the joint is normal, but as time passes attacks occur more frequently and each may last longer and affect more joints. In about half the cases, chronic gout eventually supervenes and this is characterised by the formation of gouty tophi. These are deposits of uric acid crystals which may be found in any of the structures within or around the joint. It is the presence of tophi that causes the erosions typical of the condition in the skeleton.

Gouty erosions are usually round or oval in shape and are often in the long axis of the bone. The lesions are asymmetrical and the feet are more frequently involved than the rest of the skeleton; in the majority of cases the first metatarso-phalangeal joint is involved. The lesions appear to be punched out with overhanging edges and the x-ray appearances generally show that there is sclerosis around the margin of the joint but there is no osteoporosis of the adjacent bone as with some other erosive arthropathies.

Gout has been found in skeletal assemblages from virtually all periods although the sum total described is not great. There is strong genetic element in gout but toxic factors may also be important. The disease became very common during the eighteenth century and the cartoonists of the day enjoyed depicting the red-cheeked, boozy squire with his wrapped gouty foot on a foot stool. It is possible that

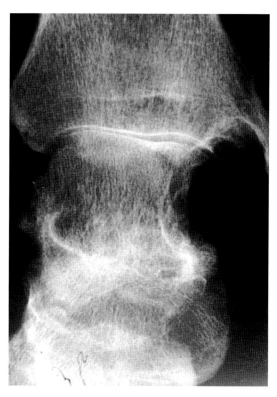

27 *Radiograph of ankle of a Roman-British skeleton with gout. The massive erosion is seen in the distal tibia and talus with an overhanging spike of bone known as a Martel hook*

the squires were suffering from one of the effects of lead poisoning. One feature of lead poisoning is kidney damage which may impair the excretion of uric acid. The wine bottles used in the eighteenth century were cleaned with lead shot and it has been suggested that some of the shot might have been caught in the gutter around the bottom of the bottle and some chemical analysis of eighteenth-century wine did indeed show that it contained a high concentration of lead, old Canary wine as much as 1,900 micrograms/litre.[12]

The effects of joint disease

Bone specialists are reluctant to neglect speculating how the diseases which they find may have affected the individuals concerned. Modern clinical experience may be helpful in understanding what the effects of particular conditions may have been, but in this part of the BS work, imagination frequently outruns medical knowledge.

We can be secure in saying that most patients with advanced erosive arthropathies would be incapacitated to some extent. Many of these conditions are painful and frequently other parts of the body are also affected and reactive arthropathy may be a sequel to serious intestinal disease. Rheumatoid arthritis and PA may leave the hands extremely disabled and the function of other joints may also be impaired but they are often not painful. In RA the first two cervical vertebrae may dislocate on sudden movement of the head because the odontoid peg has become severely eroded. This can cause compression of the spinal cord with serious neurological consequences — the patient has, in effect, a hangman's fracture. Gout may be painful in all its manifestations, although acute episodes are by far the most painful.

Joints affected by OA are painful but there is no direct relationship between the degree of pain and the changes within the joint. Joints with massive osteophyte formation may be much less painful than others with far less impressive pathology. The tendency to assume that a joint with masses of osteophyte or eburnation would have been more painful than one with fewer changes should resolutely be resisted.

The changes in an arthritic joint are sometimes described as 'severe' although this term should be confined to the descriptions of symptoms on which the BS is in no position to comment. It is sometimes obvious where osteophyte around the margin of the joint has limited movement in the joint and it is then possible to determine how the limb would have been held and from that, how the mobility of the individual may have been affected. In most matters relating to severity, the most reliable comment is none at all.

9 Infectious diseases

I have mentioned some of the infectious diseases, which might have contributed to death, in an earlier chapter, and in this chapter I will discuss their pathology and their origins a little further.

Tuberculosis

Tuberculosis as it affects man, is caused by one of two organisms, *Mycobacterium tuberculosis* and *M. bovis*,[1] and the two forms of the disease are different in some important ways. The human form of the disease is an airborne disease and the bacterium first settles out in the upper part of the lungs where it may produce a small lesion which is asymptomatic. In many cases the lesion becomes calcified and on this account it may be discovered incidentally on a chest x-ray. After a variable latent period, the primary lesion may become active and bacteria spread to other parts of the lung, the lymph nodes in the chest and to other parts of the body, including the skeleton. The infection is chronic and characterised by structures within the infected tissues in which the bacteria are surrounded by large, multinucleated cells. These structures are referred to as tubercles and they gradually replace normal tissue as the disease progresses.

Bovine tuberculosis is contracted by ingesting infected milk or other dairy products. The bacteria are absorbed from the gut and enter the abdominal lymph nodes from where they may spread throughout the lymphatic system or more widely. Bovine tuberculosis does not spread from human to human; among cattle, it is spread as a droplet infection and is primarily as disease of the lungs.

Both forms of tuberculosis may involve the bones or joints but in not more than about 35% of cases. It was formerly considered that skeletal involvement was present only in bovine tuberculosis but reference to the early literature on the disease, when it was much more common than nowadays, suggests that anything between 40-97% of cases of skeletal tuberculosis were due to the human form of the disease.

Any bone or joint may become involved but the spine is affected most frequently, usually the lower half; in children the bones of the hands are often affected and this condition is known as tuberculous dactylitis. The disease leads to the erosion and destruction of normal bone tissue. In the spine the anterior parts of the vertebrae are affected and the destruction which follows may cause the spine to collapse leading to an

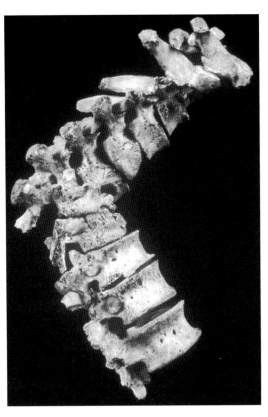

acute angulation of the spine which is referred to as Pott's disease. One feature of skeletal tuberculosis is that the erosion is not accompanied by the formation of new bone and this may be helpful when making the diagnosis, which can otherwise present great difficulty. Dan Morse and his colleagues wrote more than thirty years ago that:

> If one were to attempt to make a diagnosis [of tuberculosis] from a dried bone specimen, the only chance of making even a good guess would be on the basis of involvement of the spine; bone tuberculosis in other locations would be indistinguishable from too many other diseases.[2]

28 Spinal column from an individual with tuberculosis, showing vertebral collapse and wedging of vertebrae

Not much has changed in the interim and some more recent authors have produced a list of 19 conditions with which skeletal tuberculosis may be confused. The disease with which it most likely to be confused is brucellosis. This is another disease contracted from animals — most likely cattle in this country — by contact with infected blood such as may occur when helping a cow in labour. There seems no reason to suppose that brucellosis was not present in ancient herds of cattle or that those who tended them would not contract it. The estimate of how often brucellosis spreads to the skeleton varies from 1-75% but there is general agreement that the spine, particularly the lumbar spine, is commonly affected and the radiological and morphological appearances are similar to tuberculosis except that the formation of new bone is more common in brucellosis.

Pott's disease is a distinctive condition and cases have been recorded from antiquity, indeed it was one of the first diseases to appear in the palaeopathological literature, being described in 1910 by Elliot Smith and Ruffer. The number of cases, however, is relatively small, especially when one considers that the disease was likely to have been common in the past. The conclusion must be that the prevalence of tuberculosis in past populations has been greatly underestimated. There are two possible explanations for this. The first relates to difficulties in diagnosis. As noted above, probably no more than a third of all cases would develop skeletal lesions and then the only certain way of diagnosing the disease in the skeleton on morphological grounds depends on finding the classic spinal changes. These develop in no more that half the patients with skeletal tuberculosis and so it is easy to see why any estimates of the prevalence of tuberculosis in the past will be substantially too low, but this may not be the case in the future.

It is now possible to extract aDNA derived from *M. tuberculosis* and other organisms using the polymerase chain reaction (PCR). Moreover it is also possible to differentiate between *M. tuberculosis* and *bovis* so that not only can the diagnosis be confirmed by this method, but the infective agent can also be characterised.[3] Another technique also promises to be extremely helpful in establishing the epidemiology of the disease. Mycobacteria have a waxy coat which contains mycolic acids. These compounds can be extracted from the tissues of patients with tuberculosis and used to differentiate between strains of mycobacteria. The technique uses gas chromatography and is straightforward and much more likely than PCR to be applicable on a large scale. It is also less susceptible to

29 *Mummy with tuberculosis described by Elliot Smith and Ruffer. The angulation of the spine (Pott's disease) is clearly seen*

contamination than the analysis of aDNA and has already been used to demonstrate the presence of *M. tuberculosis* in a fragment of calcified pleura some 1,400 years old.[4] Mycolic acid analysis or PCR could be used to determine the prevalence of tuberculosis on a cemetery wide basis, although of the two, mycolic acid analysis is more likely to be used on the grounds of cost. Finding mycolic acids or bacterial aDNA in skeletons with no morphological evidence of tuberculosis would give a much better indication of the frequency of the disease in the past, but with either method, false negative results would be certain to occur, so that some underestimation of the true prevalence is still likely.

30 Cervical and thoracic spine from a young boy with tuberculosis from the Byzantine period in Turkey. The spine has collapsed in the lower cervical and upper thoracic regions and the lower thoracic vertebrae has come round to fuse with the cervical. The boy's head would have been to the left. It is hard to imagine how he survived with such a deformity. The diagnosis was confirmed by the extraction of aDNA from the bone

The use of PCR would come into its own in determining the origins of human tuberculosis. The conventional hypothesis is that tuberculosis was contracted from cattle and that over the centuries the bovine bacterium mutated into the human form; the bovine form is thought to have evolved from a saprophytic soil bacteria. Tuberculosis is rare in wild animals which are not in contact with domesticated animals although some strains do cause epizootics in wild animals. The disease occurs in a wide range of domesticated animals and in wild animals kept in captivity, and it was probably only when animals were kept in close proximity that the acute form was able to develop because close proximity readily permits airborne spread. *M. bovis* infects an exceptionally wide range of hosts, including goats, cats, dogs, pigs, buffalo, badgers, deer and bison, and it is possible that the disease spread to humans from other animals with which early man came into contact. To date, only the human mycobacterium has been recovered from human remains, so at present the jury is out.

Leprosy

Leprosy is also caused by a mycobacterium, *M. leprae*, and there is some cross immunity between *M. leprae* and *M. tuberculosis* such that tuberculosis confers immunity to leprosy, a point I will return to later. Leprosy is one of few diseases in which the study of human remains has made a significant contribution to our understanding of the disease and prompted work with infected patients. The work was carried out by Vilhelm Møller-Christensen who examined bones from four medieval leper hospital cemeteries, a total of almost 1,000 graves in all and gave the first comprehensive account of the skeletal lesions in this disease.[5]

As with tuberculosis, the clinical course in leprosy is determined by the immunological reaction invoked in the infected individual. Having gained entry to the body, the leprosy bacteria are carried to the peripheral nerves. If the infected person has good resistance the disease is confined to the nerves, producing what is known as the tuberculoid form of the disease. On the other hand, if resistance is poor, the bacteria spread to other tissues to produce the lepromatous form.[6] Skeletal changes may occur in both types of leprosy but they are much more common in the lepromatous form. Bone changes occur in the skull, the hands and the feet. The changes in the hands and the feet are the result of a number of different factors, some of which — repeated trauma and secondary infection — are due to loss of sensation, while others are due to the spread of bacteria to the bones via the blood stream.

There is a great loss of bone in leprosy but little if any bone production unless secondary infection supervenes. In the hands the distal phalanges are absorbed, together with the other phalanges as the disease progresses and the fingers become shortened to produce what is sometimes called a 'mitten hand'. The tarsal bones in the feet are absorbed, and because of damage to the sensory nerves, soft tissue damage and secondary infection are common. With advanced sensory loss the joints of the feet may be wrecked and the final picture may be extremely complex.

The changes in the skull in leprosy affect the nose and mouth and are very characteristic, and in a full-blown case, the disease is unmistakable. The anterior nasal spine is absorbed and the nasal cavity is round and wide; the alveolar margin is also eroded and there is often a loss of the front teeth. There is inflammatory change affecting the hard palate with thinning, pitting and perforation. Møller-Christensen refers to the changes in the skull as *facies leprosa*.

Leprosy is spread by direct contact, but contrary to popular belief it has a low infectivity and the disease is contracted only by close contact with infected individuals for long periods. The origins of leprosy are obscure but it may have arisen in the Far East from contact with water buffalo who commonly have a form of leprosy which affects the skin. The use of buffalo skins for clothing may have provided the contact necessary for human infection. Quite when the disease arose, however, is unknown and its mode of geographical spread is also uncertain. There is a general belief that it was brought to

Europe from the Holy Land by returning crusaders, but it existed long before that; a skeleton from the Romano-British site at Poundbury, for example, has been found with changes in the feet, almost certainly caused by leprosy.[7] Nevertheless, the disease did become more common in the medieval period and hundreds of leper hospitals were established throughout Britain and Europe. Those with leprosy were ostracised and denied normal human contact, almost certainly because of the fear that the soft tissue changes invoked, especially those affecting the face. Why the disease became more common in the medieval period has yet to be explained. Certainly not all those who were stigmatised with the disease had leprosy and even allowing for the poor standards of hygiene during the medieval period, low infectivity should have kept the disease from spreading widely.

And then it disappeared. The leprosy hospitals gradually closed and although pockets of the disease remained, especially in northern Europe, by the sixteenth century it had become a rarity. The decline of the disease has been linked with the increase in the number of cases of human tuberculosis which are supposed to have occurred during the medieval period. Infection with tuberculosis confers immunity to leprosy and it is thought that the spread of tuberculosis through the community brought about the decline in leprosy. While this theory seems plausible, it has never been confirmed and will not be until some means comes available to determine the prevalence of the two conditions with some precision.

Syphilis

Syphilis is caused by infection with the *Treponema pallidum* and is one of four diseases caused by treponemal infection. Of the others, pinta is a skin disease and both yaws and endemic syphilis (bejal) affect the skeleton. The skeletal lesions in the treponematoses cannot readily be distinguished on morphological grounds, although a reasonable inference as to which is present can be made on the origin of the specimens.

The changes in syphilis (as I will now refer exclusively to the venereal form) are most commonly seen in the skull and the tibia and result from reaction to the presence of the infective organisms which produces a cycle of erosion and proliferation. In the skull, the changes generally start in the frontal bone and the earliest lesions are pits on the surface of the bone which may become confluent and cavitated. The edges of the cavitated areas become raised and roll over the margins of the lesion and, as healing proceeds, the wall and base of the cavity are covered until only a shallow depression remains with radial scarring on the surface. The successive erosion and healing produces an absolutely characteristic appearance, and was called *caries sicca* by Cecil Hackett whose classic description of syphilis in dried bones still forms the basis for diagnosis.[8] The nasal bones, nasal septum, palate and the structures with the nose are often involved, and destroyed by spread from the nasal mucosa. In a skull, the nasal

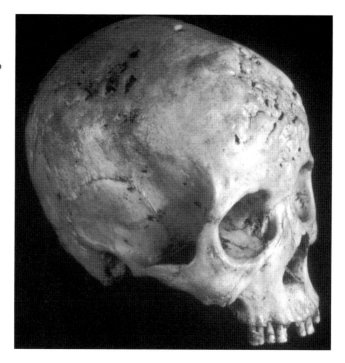

31 Skull with stigmata of syphilis on frontal bones. Courtesy of San Diego Museum of Man

cavity may appear empty and enlarged as in leprosy, but the anterior nasal spine is generally spared in syphilis.

Syphilitic involvement of the extra-cranial skeleton leads to the proliferation of new bone on sub-cutaneous surfaces. The tibia is by far the most favoured site for extra-cranial syphilis, and it becomes swollen and heavy and may appear to be bowed by the apposition of new bone on the anterior surface. There is a form of congenital syphilis in which the foetus is infected *in utero* and then the laying down of new bone on the front of the tibia may be so great that it is referred to as a sabre tibia.

The treponemal diseases are closely related and their expression seems to be dictated by environmental conditions. Thus pinta is found in South and Central America, yaws is a disease of the wet tropic and endemic syphilis of dry, arid regions. This may represent the trail of evolution, with its likely origin a monkey treponeme.

In 1530, Girolamo Fracastoro published a poem entitled *Syphilis sive morbus Gallicus* (Syphilis or the French disease). In it, Syphilis, a rich young shepherd, is inflicted with a loathsome disease for insulting the god Apollo. Fracastoro was writing in the wake of the outbreak of an epidemic of syphilis throughout Europe, the symptoms of which were elegantly described in his poem. What caused the sudden outbreak of what seemed to be a new disease has never been satisfactorily determined, but it has become customary to blame Columbus and his sailors for importing it from the New World. Columbus returned from his voyage to America in 1493 and some years later a Spanish physician stated that some of his sailors had suffered from syphilis. A counter-claim has it that the true state of affairs is that Columbus and his sailors imported the disease into the New

World rather than exporting it from there, while a third state of affairs is proposed in which the disease was present concurrently in both the Old and New Worlds and Columbus took it nowhere.

It beggars belief that the crew of a small sailing ship could propagate a disease which spread throughout the whole of Europe within a few months of their landing; sexually active they may have been, but surely not *that* active. It seems much more likely that there was coincidentally a change in the parasite-host relationship which caused the infection to become more virulent in Europe, and that syphilis co-existed in the Old World and the New. Several skeletons with syphilis have now been found in various parts of Europe which seems finally to put paid to the Columbian hypothesis.[9] The issue which is taxing BS now is diagnosing which of the three treponemal diseases which affects bone was occurring where and when, and if an answer can be found this will contribute greatly to our understanding of the natural history and evolution of these diseases.

10 Trauma and treatment

Fighting and brawling are concomitants of the human condition, the consequences of an aggressive nature which was not substantially ameliorated by the discovery of alcohol. In any collection of human remains there are skeletons with signs of trauma, the most common being fractured bones. The type of injury may be inferred from the appearance of the fracture and whether or not the injured person received any sort of medical treatment.

Fractures

There are many kinds of fracture some descriptive or radiological and some surgical (see **Table 12**). Transverse fractures occur as the result of force applied at right angles to the long axis of the bone, such as might occur from a heavy blow. A spiral fracture is the result of abnormal force applied radially to the long axis and is the type commonly seen nowadays in skiing accidents where the foot becomes trapped and the force of the body violently twists the leg, resulting in a spiral fracture of the tibia and fibula. Compression or crush fractures occur when force is applied to the bone from two sides; this type of fracture may occur in the vertebrae as the result of a fall, for example. A greenstick fracture only occurs in children in whom the bones are much more elastic than in adults. When force is applied the bone bends slightly and the cortex on the outside of the bend splits in the same way that a green stick cracks when it is bent. A simple fracture is one in which there is a single break and the skin is unbroken; when the skin is broken the fracture is said to be compound. A comminuted fracture is one in which the bone is broken into several pieces; it may also be compound. When the fracture line extends into a joint it is said to be intra-articular. Finally, a pathological fracture is the result of pathological change in the bone — secondary spread of a tumour, for example — and may occur with minimal trauma.

When a bone breaks, the distal end of the broken bone is displaced upwards by the violent contraction of the muscles around the break; there is invariably some soft tissue damage which may involve blood vessels or nerves around the fracture, and there is loss of blood into the tissues. In order that the bone heals well it is essential to reduce the fracture, that is, put the broken ends of the bone back into their normal anatomical position so far as is possible, and then immobilise it. In some situations, broken bones may

Table 12 Description of major types of fracture

Type of fracture	Description
Simple (closed) fracture	One in which the skin remains intact
Compound (open) fracture	One in which the bone communicates with the outside environment; the bone may or may not protrude through the skin
Complete fracture	One in which the entire circumference of a tubular bone, or both surfaces of a flat bone, have been disrupted
Incomplete fracture	One in which the break does not extend completely through the bone
Transverse, oblique, transverse-oblique, spiral fracture	Description of line of force causing disruption of bone
Comminuted fracture	One with two or more fragments
Impaction fracture	One in which one fragment is driven into the opposing fragment
Depression fracture	One in which the cortex of the bone is driven into underlying softer bone
Crush fracture	One caused by compression forces
Stress fracture	One caused by repeated cyclical load; may occur in normal or pathological bone
Pathological fracture	One occuring through an are of abnormal bone
Greenstick fracture	One occurring in immature bone affecting one cortex only

be naturally splinted and therefore are not displaced. Fractured ribs need no immobilisation (unless there is massive injury to the chest), nor does a fractured radius or ulna provided the other is intact, and nor does a fractured fibula if the tibia is intact. The time taken to repair a fractured bone is variable; it takes much less time in the young than in the elderly, but in general, union takes 4-8 weeks and a further 4-6 weeks may be necessary before the limb is fully serviceable.

Healing takes place in a series of well-recognised stages. First, the blood clot which forms around the broken ends organises itself and a type of woven bone called callus is formed in it and the broken ends of the bone start to remodel and become rounded. The immature bone in the callus is gradually replaced by mature bone and remodelled to restore the original shape and the marrow cavity is recanalised. The site of the fracture may be visible for years after the injury, but in some cases the fracture may be so perfectly healed that no trace remains of it after only a year.

32 Depressed fracture of the skull caused by a blow to the head. Courtesy of San Diego Museum of Man

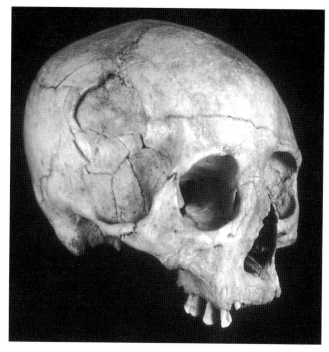

There are many complications of fractures of which the first to consider is non-union. The most usual cause for non-union is that the fracture is not immobilised during healing, but soft tissue such as fat or muscle may intervene between the two broken ends of the bone when it is fractured, and if so the bone cannot unite properly. Where non-union occurs, the bones are held together by fibrous tissue forming what is known as a pseudarthrosis, but the function of the limb is usually impaired to some extent. In some cases, the blood supply to one of the broken elements may be impaired or cut off altogether, and the part deprived of its nutrition may undergo avascular necrosis. The head of the femur is especially prone to avascular necrosis when the neck of the femur is fractured because the arteries which supply the head enter into the hip joint through the capsule of the joint. If the capsule is damaged by the injury then the blood supply to the head of the femur is compromised and the head is resorbed over the next few months. The stump of the neck comes to articulate with the acetabulum or the outer surface of the ilium if the hip joint has also been disarticulated to form a pseudarthrosis which is easily recognised in the skeleton.

Injuries to blood vessels may occur when a bone is fractured and may lead to a loss of muscle function or to gangrene in extreme cases. Nerves which are close to the site of the fracture may also be damaged with resultant paralysis of the muscles supplied by them, or sensory loss. Another serious complication of a fracture is secondary infection; this is a much more likely event with a compound fracture and may result in osteomyelitis or tetanus if soil or other foreign material gets into the wound. Infection may not only delay healing, or prevent it altogether, but it may lead to the death of the injured person.

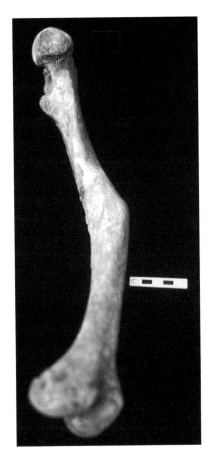

33 Healed fracture of the femur with considerable angulation of the shaft

What is striking about fractured bones in skeletal assemblages is that the majority are well-healed and in good alignment, and the prevalence of secondary infection appears to be very low. This can only mean that from very early times there existed a body of knowledge — or individuals with this knowledge — of the importance of reducing fractures and immobilising them during the healing period. Reducing a fractured femur in the days before anaesthesia and adequate analgesia must have been a trying experience for patient and practitioner alike, and no doubt involved copious amounts of alcohol, some even for the patient. The knowledge of splinting is very old indeed and Elliot Smith and Wood Jones found skeletons with splints applied to broken bones during their work in Nubia in the early 1900s.[1] It is important to restore the proper alignment of a fracture since otherwise the limb will not function well and there is a high probability that the joints around the limb will develop osteoarthritis; if a fracture extends into a joint, then osteoarthritis is almost inevitable because the mechanics of the joint will be irretrievably altered.

Quite how and when the knowledge of how to treat fractures was acquired we do not know. Surgery was taught at the medieval universities — at Bologna, Palermo and Montpellier, for example — and surgical procedures are illustrated in some extant manuscripts but surgery was not for the common mass of people who would presumably have had access instead to bone setters. Knowledge of bone setting is found among many modern indigenous people and some have developed ingenious methods for reducing and immobilising fractures.[2] The study of human bones can demonstrate that the knowledge is ancient but can give no clues as to its origins.

The other factor required for the successful healing of a fracture is some kind of social support system whereby the injured person can be cared for during the time that the bone is healing and in the convalescent period afterwards.[3] Perhaps the instinct to care for injured members of our species has extremely ancient roots, derived even from primate ancestors since there are several instances where primates in the wild have been found with healed fractures. A primate with a fractured arm or leg is unable to fend for themselves and one supposes that they too would at least have been fed while their injuries were healing.

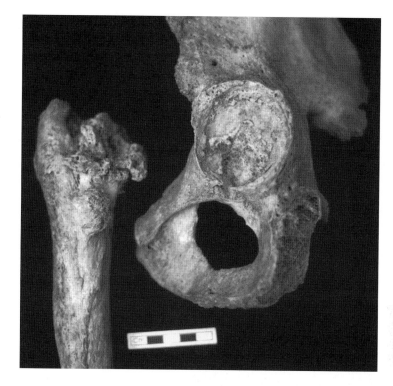

34 Fractured neck of the femur with avascular necrosis of the head and development of secondary osteoarthritis

Autopsy and amputation

Reducing and treating fractures is one form of medical treatment which can be inferred from the study of human remains; others include evidence for autopsy and amputation.

Autopsy

The dissection of the human body was carried out in the first instance for magico-religious reasons and although some knowledge of anatomy would thereby have been obtained — those in charge of mummification in Egypt would have been conversant with the shape and arrangement of the abdominal viscera, for example — this was not the purpose of the procedure, and it is likely that butchers would have had a better working knowledge of anatomy than anyone else, at least until the Graeco-Roman period. The Alexandrian Greeks dissected the body and Celsus, writing in the first century AD, asserts that it was necessary to study the cadaver in order to gain knowledge of anatomy.

Throughout the Middles Ages there are sporadic references to autopsy but the procedure was hampered if not actually forbidden by the attitude of the Church. The decree promulgated at the Council of Tours in 1163 that *Ecclesia abhorret a sanguine* was widely interpreted to mean that the clergy should not perform surgery either on the living or the dead. In 1299, Pope Boniface VIII forbade the cooking of bodies to separate the flesh from the bones, a practice used to bring home the bodies of some of those who died in the Crusades. Although the ban was specific in its instructions, many considered that it

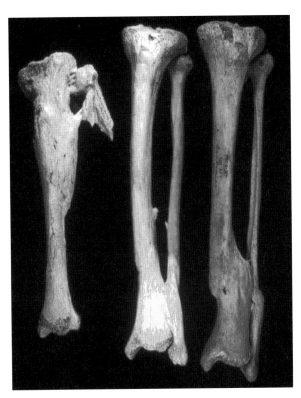

35 Three healed spiral fractures of the lower leg. Courtesy of San Diego Museum of Man

also prohibited dissection. The Church's attitude notwithstanding, post-mortem examinations *were* undertaken, although usually for forensic reasons.

By the end of the thirteenth century in England, autopsies were a sufficiently common practice that one is illustrated in a manuscript which describes a gynaecological case in which the patient has been eviscerated and her organs displayed around the edge of the illustration. Anatomy textbooks of the medieval period show dissection taking place but the study of anatomy was held back by the deference shown to the ancients, particularly to Galen, whose anatomy held chief place. It is doubtful whether Galen dissected a body, and his descriptions are based on dissections of pigs, but during the Middles Ages, if dissection of the body showed that the disposition of the organs was different from the way in which Galen described them, then the body was wrong and not Galen. The publication of Vesalius's *De corporis humani fabrica* in 1543, with its wonderful woodcuts by Stephan von Calcar who had been a pupil of Titian, finally overthrew the Galenic system of anatomy and established it on a modern footing. The practice of autopsy increased particularly throughout the eighteenth and nineteenth centuries when it formed the basis of pathology first in England, then France and Austria.

Evidence for autopsies is not uncommon in human remains recovered from eighteenth- or nineteenth-century contexts, mostly carried out one assumes for pathological rather than anatomical reasons. The pathognomonic sign that an autopsy has been carried out is the removal of the calvarium by a saw cut which extends straight around the skull some 2cm or so above the orbits. The operator often had to take two or three attempts to get his saw to grip and a number of failed cuts can often be seen. On other occasions, the saw cut does not extend completely around the skull and the skull cap is lifted up from the front and broken off at the back, leaving a small flange of bone sticking up above the rim. Children and adults were subject to post-mortem examination. In some cases it is clear from the presence of saw cuts on the ribs that the contents of the chest were examined and the spinal cord was taken out for study in other cases as shown by the removal of the laminae of the vertebrae.

Unfortunately we cannot tell what decided whether or not an autopsy was carried out in a particular case since there is almost never any indication of the cause of death. Nevertheless, finding clear evidence of an autopsy can contribute to the history of the procedure itself as securely dated remains may help to confirm when it became well established.

Amputation

Evidence for amputation among human remains is rare until the eighteenth century, which was in some respects the heroic age of surgery. Battle surgeons have no doubt resorted to amputation for centuries, and in some eras amputation was meted out as a punishment for certain types of crime, and some peoples amputated fingers for ritualistic reasons, sometimes causing substantial mutilation to their hands.

In the eighteenth century we have several detailed accounts of how the operation was carried out. The patient would be placed on a wooden table and held down by three or four assistants while the surgeon began his work with knife and saw. A cut was made through the skin and muscles leaving a flap of skin to be sewn over the wound. The bone was sawn through with two or three cuts, the arteries tied, the flap sutured in place, and the patient returned to his bed. Some surgeons could remove a leg in less than a minute.

36 Cross section of femur showing amputation marks and small, raised triangle of bone. This shows that the surgeon cut in two directions to remove the leg

Robert Liston who was a surgeon at University College Hospital in London was renowned for the speed with which he worked. It was said of him that

> Amputations were his special delight
> and . . . in his hands the use of the
> saw followed the flash of the knife so
> quickly that the student who turned
> his head for even a moment found
> that the amputation was completed
> when he looked round again.[4]

If the student did not get his hands out of the way during the procedure he might also find he had lost a finger or two when he looked round.

37 Distal femur and proximal tibia and fibula. The lower leg was amputated but the individual survived sufficiently long for the tibia and fibular to remodel

The chances that the patient would survive the operation were slim, for if they did not die of shock on the table, then they would have to take their chance with septicaemia after their wound had become infected, which it invariably did before Lister introduced his antiseptic carbolic spray in 1870. The remains of those who had had amputations confirm that many died before any appreciable healing had taken place; conversely, some individuals certainly survived long after the operation as the cut bones are healed and remodelled.

With some amputations the bone proximal to the amputation survives; in other cases, the distal part of the limb is recovered. Some details of the technique used to cut the bone can be gained from looking at the cut surface which will show the striations caused by the teeth of the saw (the kerf) and — almost always — a small piece of bone left when the bone snapped. The actual number of cuts taken to sever the bone can be determined from this piece of bone since it has as many straight sides as cuts.

Amputations are found in individuals of all ages but in no case that I have seen was there any indications of the underlying disease. The conditions for which amputations were carried out would have included compound fractures, osteomyelitits, aneurysm of the popliteal artery, gangrene, bone and soft tissue tumours, congenital anomalies and advanced joint disease, but many of these would leave no signs on the surviving skeleton. Some conjectures can be made, however. Finding a below knee amputation in association with healed fractures in the other parts of the skeleton may suggest that the individual had an accident in which he sustained a compound fracture of the tibia. In a young person, on the other hand, a mid-thigh amputation could suggest that the operation had been carried out to remove a sarcoma at the knee. The distal fragment ought to be more informative — in theory — and some survive from hospital sites. One lower leg of a juvenile which was recovered from a hospital site in Gloucester seemed normal in all respects. The foot was missing so it is possible that it had a lesion which necessitated the operation, although it is difficult to believe that a disease of the foot would have required a mid-thigh amputation. More likely there was a soft tissue lesion around the knee but the bones give no idea of its nature, supposing it had existed at all.

An eighteenth-century anatomy school uncovered

During building work at 36 Craven Street, next to Charing Cross Station in London, some human remains were found in the basement. The house had been occupied by Benjamin Franklin who lived in London between 1757 and 1775 when he was agent for some of the American colonies. In 1772 Franklin moved to 7 Craven Street and the house was occupied by William Hewson. Hewson was an anatomist and had been a student of William Hunter and was a partner in Hunter's anatomy school in Windmill Street. After a quarrel with his partner, Hewson set up his own anatomy school in Craven Street. Hewson died from septicaemia in 1774 as the result of dissecting a decomposed corpse, and his school and his collection of specimens was left to his assistant, Magnus Falconer, who himself died in 1777 from tuberculosis. Some of the specimens from the anatomy school were bought by William and John Hunter and these have been preserved in the Hunterian Museums in London and Glasgow.

The refuse from the school was excavated from a pit in the basement and contained human remains with a wide variety of cuts, but also the bones of dogs, birds, fish and turtles and well as glassware and other materials. The human remains included those from children and adults, and skulls which had been drilled in several places using a trephine; some had multiple holes suggesting they had been used to practice the technique of trepanation (see below). Some of the cuts on the long bones were made to demonstrate anatomical relations in the limbs but some may also have been practice amputations. The Craven Street site is unique and provides an opportunity to study the procedures, materials and equipment used in a private anatomy school during an important period of the development of anatomy, and further study of the remains will be valuable for historians and palaeopathologists alike.[5]

Battered babies

In modern Britain at least one child in a thousand under the age of four suffers severe physical abuse, including fractures, brain haemorrhage, internal injuries or mutilation, and the mortality rate of such children is at least one in 10,000. Child abuse is often

Table 13 Peak times of morphological or radiological appearances of fractures in children.
[†]A fracture without periosteal new bone is usually less than 7–10 days old and seldom more than 20 days. A fracture with only slight periosteal new bone formation could be only 4–7 days old

Morphological or radiological appearance	Time from occurence of fracture
Periosteal new bone formation[†]	10-14 days
Loss of definition of fracture line	14-21 days
Soft callus formation	14-21 days
Hard callus formation	21-42 days
Remodelling	1 year

spoken of as a modern phenomenon but there is plenty of documentary evidence that it has a long and undistinguished history. Soranus of Ephesus writing in the early second century AD was aware that infants might be neglected or abused. In his *Gynaecology* he gives advice on choosing a wet nurse and comments that she should be self-controlled, sympathetic and affectionate. Angry women, he writes,

> are like maniacs and sometimes when the newborn cries from fear and they are unable to restrain it, they let it drop from their hands and overturn it dangerously.[6]

The Arab physician Rhazes, who is the author of what is considered to be the earliest surviving treatise on paediatrics, was aware that some injuries in children may be caused intentionally. There seems no reason to suppose, therefore, that human nature has altered in any important respect in the last two thousand years, or that it is only in recent times that adults have treated children cruelly, yet in no skeletal assemblage that I have examined — and in which children account for up to a quarter of the total population — has a single case been found in which the death could have been attributed to wilful abuse.

The criteria by which child abuse may be recognised have been described many times by paediatricians and radiologists. In addition to the soft tissue signs of trauma, which are not available to BS, there are some well-recognised radiological signs that can guide those who examine children's skeletons. The most revealing indication of deliberate harm is the presence of multiple fractures at different stages of healing, indicating that they have occurred over a length of time (see **Table 13**). Fractures of the ribs are common in abused children and they may also be found in ribs, sternum, vertebrae and skull.

The radiological signs can easily be recognised in the skeleton. Kerley has recorded the case of three infants who were killed by their parents and buried in the basement and back yard of the house. The case came to light when two children who were being interviewed by their teacher as to the number of siblings they had, casually remarked that there had been three more of them but that their mother and father had killed them.[7] Multiple fractures, some healed and some healing, were found in the skeletons of all three children, the sites affected including the mandible, ribs, clavicle, radius and ulna; the left clavicle of one of the children had two separate fractures. In addition to these fractures, Kerley noted some which he considered had been caused at or around the time of death, and there were also breaks which had occurred during excavation; the latter could be distinguished by the fact that the broken ends of the bones were of a lighter colour than the surface.

All three skeletons that Kerley examined had unequivocal evidence of ante-mortem fractures in various stages of healing and which had certainly be caused at different times in the children's lives, confirming that they had been subject to repeated trauma. Kerley stressed the importance of x-raying suspected fractures as the increased density at the broken ends is evidence of remodelling and a sure sign that the fracture occurred before death. While this might be a requirement in a forensic case, an experienced BS could hardly fail to differentiate an ante-mortem from a peri-mortem fracture, nor confuse a true fracture with a break which had occurred during excavation.

It is unlikely that the sort of injuries that would be sustained by a battered child would escape notice among a burial assemblage although children who die as the result of abuse may be buried clandestinely, as happened in Kerley's case. So where are these abused children in the archaeological record? The likely answer is to do with numbers. Modern data suggest that although approximately 0.4% of children suffer abuse, the mortality rate is only about one in ten thousand, and in those who survive the injuries will heal and bones will remodel, and if they survive into adulthood, there will be no skeletal evidence to show that they were harmed when they were children. If the rates of child abuse in the past are at all comparable with those of the present day, the chances of finding an abused infant are small. Thus the apparent absence of battered babies among skeletal assemblages is most likely to be a statistical artefact and cannot be taken as evidence that the abuse of children did not occur. Even if the skeletons of abused children were to be discovered, the true prevalence of abuse would be a substantial underestimate, as the majority of those who suffer intentional harm survive, and the evidence vanishes as their skeleton matures and remodels.

Trephination

Trephination is an operation which has an extremely long history and seems to have been practised worldwide. The operation consists of removing a piece of the calvarium without damage to the underlying blood vessels, meninges or brain. A number of techniques have been used including scraping, grooving, boring, cutting and rectangular intersecting incisions. In all cases the scalp would have been incised and reflected back from the skull to give the operator a clear view; this would probably have been achieved with an X-shaped cut. After the operation, the skull flaps would be replaced and either be allowed to

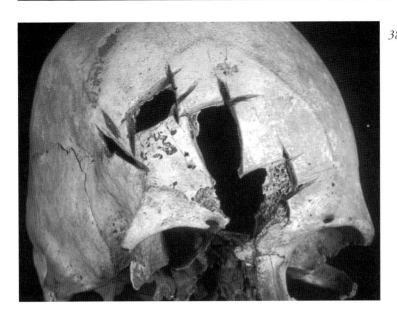

38 Skull showing the results of several trephinations. These may have been made after death by 'surgeons' during training. Courtesy of San Diego Museum of Man

granulate up or be held together with sutures or by some other method. Most trephinations are found in the frontal or parietal bones, thus avoiding the superior sagittal sinus which runs along the midline. Those who undertook the operation must have known that damage to the sinus would result in massive haemorrhage and death. This knowledge presumably came as the result of trial and error; it would quickly have become obvious that operating in the mid-line was not likely to be in the patient's best interests, and this information would have been passed on from one generation of operator to the next.

The earliest trephinations were carried out with stone tools, but later instruments were made of bronze or iron, and much later, the trephine was introduced which had a circular blade for removing a roundel of bone. These instruments were in use until comparatively recently for removing bone to remove a subdural haematoma, for example.

Many examples of trephinations have been recovered, and in a good many cases it seems that the patients survived for some while after the operation. Other skulls show evidence of secondary infection, others show the presence of more than one healed operation. Yet others have incomplete trephination where the bone has not been removed, and others have so many unhealed holes in them that it seems most likely that these skulls were used for practicing the technique. Skulls were also trephined after death to obtain roundels of skull for use as amulets.

The indications for trephination have been the subject of much discussion. One of the earliest explanations was that it was done for magico-religious reasons to let out evil spirits. There is historical and ethnographic evidence, however, that trephination was carried out for therapeutic purposes after head injuries, especially to remove depressed fractures — although it is interesting that very few trephined skulls show evidence of any other injury — and for a variety of other conditions including headaches, epilepsy and other neurological and psychological conditions. The operation is still carried out in parts of Africa and has been filmed and described by modern authors. The technique seems to have changed little over the centuries, although local anaesthetics are sometimes used, and so are often out of date antibiotics. One spectacular case was described some years ago by Edward Margetts in a 50-year-old man belonging to the Kisii tribe in Kenya. In 1940 he had hit his head on a door lintel and developed persistent headaches and had his first trephination five years later. Over the next seven or eight years he had several more operations — the number he claimed varied between five and thirty — but what *was* certain was that virtually the whole of the top of his head was missing; Margetts estimated that he had a hole about 30 square inches in his skull vault. He was apparently well, but there was so much concern about him, that he was fitted with a plastic skull cap which he wore under his everyday hat.[8]

Examination of human remains can throw no light on the reasons that this extraordinary operation was carried out but the trephined skulls bear a remarkable testament to the stoicism of those who submitted to the operation.

11 Cancer in antiquity

Modern society tends to be very parochial about the diseases which afflict it, and there is sometimes a tendency to think that no one has suffered from them before, or if they did, then not to the extent that *we* suffer. Nowhere is this more evident than in the case of cancer, which, because it is now such a common cause of death, holds a particular dread. Calvin Wells reinforced the notion that cancer is a new disease:

> It is with carcinoma that the greatest difference is found between modern and ancient patterns of malignant disease . . . Evidence of the disease from early burial grounds is rare.[1]

Wells refers specifically to carcinoma and so it perhaps worthwhile clarifying the nomenclature of malignant disease which can be confusing, especially as some of the terms are used indiscriminately. The word 'tumour', which literally means a swelling, is used to describe any kind of new growth of cells. Sometimes 'neoplasm' is used as a synonym, especially by doctors trying to hide bad news from a patient, but, as suggested, it tends to have a sinister connotation. Tumours may be either malignant or benign; malignant tumours are those which spread to other tissues or organs, whereas benign tumours remain *in situ*. Benign tumours may nevertheless be harmful as they may cause damage to other organs through pressure; benign tumours which arise inside the skull, for example, can be lethal as the result of an increase in intra-cranial pressure. Cancer is the generic term for any kind of malignant tumour.

All tumours take the suffix '-oma', prefixed by the name given to the type of tissue in which they arise. Thus carcinomas are malignant tumours arising from squamous epithelium, such as that which lines the gastro-intestinal tract or the airways. Sarcomas derive from connective tissues — muscle, bone and cartilage — and adenomas take their origin from glandular tissue. (A more comprehensive description is shown in **Table 14**.)

The skeleton is affected by tumours either directly or by secondary spread. Primary bone tumours are rare and nowadays account for about 200 deaths per year. The peak incidence is during the years of active bone growth, between the ages of 10 and 20, and boys are affected more often than girls. The favourite sites for the tumour are around the knee, the upper arm and hip, the areas of rapid bone growth. There is second peak in old age as there is a slight tendency for the disease to develop in bone affected by Paget's disease and about 1% of patients with Paget's disease develop osteosarcoma. The

Table 14 Terms used to describe tumours

Tumour	Literally, a swelling. General term for any kind of new growth
Neoplasm	Synonym for tumour, but often has sinister connotations
Benign tumour (BT)	One which does not spread to other organs or tissues. It may, however, produce harmful effects
Malignant tumour (MT)	One which spreads to other organs or tissues. The cells which spread form secondary tumours or metastases; the site of origin is referred to as the primary tumour
Cancer	Generic term for any malignant tumour
Carcinoma	MT arising from squamous epithelium
Adenoma	MT arising from glandular tissue
Sarcoma	MT arising from muscle, cartilage, bone, fibrous tissue, blood or lymph vessels
Meningioma	BT arising from meninges of brain or spinal cord
Myeloma	MT arising from plasma cells in bone marrow
Leukaemia	MT of white blood cells (does not form discrete mass)
Osteoma	Benign tumour of bone

likelihood of finding a primary bone tumour in human remains is thus small, but since they have a serious rarity value, any which are found almost always form the subject of a paper in a learned journal.

Secondary tumours account for by far the greatest number of tumours seen in bone but the various primaries show a different propensity to spread to the skeleton. Those which most commonly involve bones include carcinoma of the prostate, breast and lung. The majority of prostate cancers (60-85%) and breast cancers (60-70%) spread to bone, compared with 20-30% of lung cancers.

Secondary tumours do not spread uniformly throughout the skeleton. The most commonly involved skeletal sites include (in rank order) the vertebrae, pelvis, femur (especially the hip) and the skull; secondary bone tumours in the upper limb are much less common. The mode of spread may be through the lymphatic system, the blood stream or by direct spread.

Types of secondary spread

Most tumours that spread to bone produce lytic lesions in which bone tissue is replaced by tumour tissue. In the skeleton, all that is left is the hole which was once occupied by the abnormal tissue. The holes which are left usually vary considerably in size, have

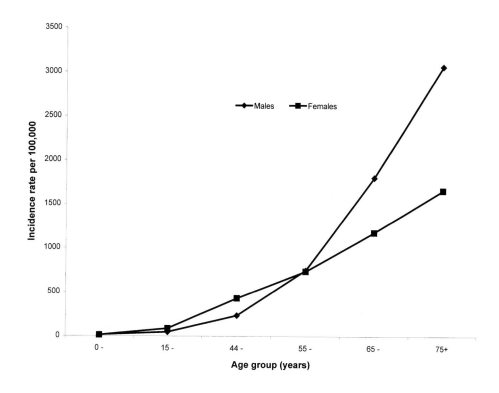

39 Number of new cases of cancer by age group. The female incidence is greater than the male at younger age groups due to the occurrence of breast cancer. The incidence in males rises much more rapidly in males after the age of 55

undercut edges and show little if any signs of healing, and there is no difficulty in distinguishing them from holes resulting from other agencies such as an excavator's pick or a bullet hole. The lesions are seen to best advantage in the vault of the skull and an x-ray will invariable show several other defects which are not apparent to the naked eye. Carcinoma of the prostate is unusual in that secondary spread induces the production of bone, and this type of secondary tumour is called a sclerosing tumour, a reference to the radiological appearance in which clouds of ill-defined new bone are seen. Lytic lesions should never be missed, even by the most inexperienced observer, but their cause requires some consideration and one should not immediately suppose that because a skeleton has holes in the skull, it is a sign of carcinoma. Other — admittedly rarer — causes need to be borne in mind, and differentiation between them may be difficult, not to say impossible in the absence of the original tumour tissue.

Causes of cancer

Cancer results from cells slipping from the normal control mechanisms which regulate their multiplication. Cells normally divide in an orderly fashion and do not extend beyond the confines of the organ of which they are a part, but cancerous cells divide and spread in a disorderly fashion. This propensity to get out of control increases markedly with age as can be seen from figure **39**. Before the age of about 55, cancer is relatively uncommon, but in the succeeding decades, the incidence increases at an exponential rate. The ultimate cause of cancer is damage to chromosomes or DNA, but what gives rise to this damage is not understood in all cases. As with all disease, the cause of cancer is either genetic, environmental or a combination of the two. Genetic in this sense refers to an inherited tendency to develop a particular type of tumour, such as happens, for example, with breast tumours which seem to run in families. Some inherited conditions in themselves carry a risk of developing cancer as happens when polyps in the colon turn malignant. Of course, what is not due to inherited factors must be due to external or environmental factors, of which the best known, not to say notorious, is smoking. There is a not very extensive list of industrial chemicals which are known or suspected or being human carcinogens, asbestos being most culpable. Otherwise, the list of known environmental carcinogens is not long but may include exposure to barbecued food, coffee, alcohol and sex. Indeed, the medical profession seems keen to put a damper on all enjoyable activities. Smoking apart, however, there are rather few modern habits or exposures which are absolutely known to be linked with cancer and it could be hypothesised that cancer is an inevitable consequence of life and although we may change the types of tumour to which we are subject, by altering lifestyle or controlling environmental or occupational exposures to chemicals, we will never escape from the disease altogether.

Cancer in past populations

By contrast with Calvin Wells, Don Brothwell wrote around the same time that

> . . . one of the points I wish to emphasize . . . is the likelihood that the scarcity of tumours has been *overemphasized* in the past — a fact which in itself may have depressed some detailed searching.[2]

Since he wrote there has been a good deal of detailed searching, many putative cases of cancer in human remains have been described and we can no longer doubt that the disease has antiquity which rivals that of man himself. The routine radiography of elderly male skeletons would be certain to increase the yield of cases of carcinoma of the prostate since in most cases the bones appear normal, except perhaps from seeming rather heavier than usual. The cases which have generally been described in the palaeopathological literature

Table 15 Estimation of upper and lower limits of prevalence of secondary cancer in the skeleton, by age and sex. See text for derivation of data

Sex	Limits	Age (years)				
		0–	15–	45–	65+	Total
Male	Upper	<0.01	0.22	0.82	0.64	1.69
	Lower	<0.01	0.08	0.30	0.24	0.63
Female	Upper	<0.01	1.36	3.93	1.70	7.00
	Lower	<0.01	0.80	2.31	0.98	4.10

are those of the much less common type in which new bone is formed on the surfaces of the bones.[3] The appearances in these cases are often spectacular and by no means to be overlooked, but it is certain that many other cases *have* been overlooked. Radiography of the post-cranial skeleton would also be likely to increase the number of secondary tumours found in the elderly of both sexes, especially where the skull is missing.

What number of cancer cases should we expect in human remains?

We can accept that cancer would have been present throughout the whole of human history, but it would be useful to calculate the likely prevalence in the past so that the numbers observed could be compared against the expected number. This might allow trends in prevalence to be studied and might also show the degree to which the prevalence is presently being underestimated.

There are no data which can be put to use before the registration of deaths became obligatory in 1837, and unfortunately the early volumes published by the Registrar General are not helpful as the causes of death are not given in detail. The 68th *Annual Report* of the Registrar General, however, gives an account of cancer deaths by site for the five years, 1901-5. Using these data as the best approximation we have to the mortality experience of early populations it is possible to calculate the number of cases of secondary cancer arising from the major primary sites. Since the proportion of primary tumours which spreads to bone is variable, estimates of the expected number can be made using the lower and the higher figures quoted in the medical literature. An estimate has to be made for each primary site and the total obtained by summing the results for each site. When this is done, it is found that less than 2% of male skeletons would be expected to show signs of secondary carcinoma, but that between 4-7% of female skeletons would be expected to do so (see **Table 15**). The comparable proportions based on modern data suggest that between 14-18% of male skeletons and 29-37% of female skeletons would show evidence of malignant disease which does indeed show that cancer is more common now than in the past. The cause of the increase in cancer in the present day is due overwhelmingly to the great increase in lung cancer in both males and females and to breast cancer in females.[4]

Diagnosing types of cancer in human remains

The origin of secondary tumours in bone can often be inferred by knowing the site of the primary tumour. Bony secondaries which occur in a woman with breast cancer are almost certainly to have arisen from her breast tumour, and similar considerations would apply to secondaries in a male with lung cancer. Where there is any doubt as to the source of bony secondaries, the tumour can be biopsied and studied under the microscope; this will provide the answer in the great majority of cases. BS looking at human remains are — as always — approaching the problem from the wrong direction, that is, starting with the hole and trying to deduce what type of tissue filled it during life. Because of this, any conclusion is going to be a best guess, with the exception of prostate cancer where the appearances are sufficiently distinctive that one can be much more secure in the diagnosis.

There are 40 or so primary sites from which tumours may spread to bone, and any BS who claimed to be able to differentiate between all 40 in the skeleton must be suspected to have access to knowledge denied to mere mortals. The site of the primary tumour may be clear from anatomical considerations; a tumour which destroys the nasal cavity, for example, is hardly likely to have arisen anywhere but in the nasopharynx. A few secondary tumours cause bones to expand, most notably carcinoma of the kidney or the thyroid, and the radiological appearances of kidney secondaries are distinct so that these features would allow a diagnosis to be made, at least on the grounds of the balance of probabilities. Otherwise it is most likely that lytic secondaries in a male have come from a lung primary, while those in a female may have come from breast or lung, and given that breast tumours were more than lung tumours in females in the past, the most probable source would be carcinoma of the breast.

What has not yet been carried out is a large-scale study of the prevalence of malignant disease in human remains. Where tumours occur they tend to be written up as single cases and not as part of a population study. The small numbers involved in any single skeletal assemblage is bound to lead to errors in determining prevalence, errors which can be reduced by combining the results of different studies. At present the most we can say about cancer in the past is that it does seem to be less common than today, but as to any trends — nothing.

12 The teeth

Teeth survive extremely well under most burial conditions and sometimes all that may be left of a body in the ground is a Cheshire cat grin when the skeleton has otherwise completely decomposed. As already seen, teeth are invaluable for ageing purposes, but they also provide evidence for dental disease and dental hygiene, and some have claimed that family relationships can be established by studying some variations in tooth structure; others have interpreted various forms of dental wear as being indicative of occupational activities.

Dental caries

Caries is the result of the production of acid by the bacteria which inhabit dental plaque. The acid produced destroys the enamel, dentine and cement, and the end result is a cavity in the crown or the root. When the dentine is attacked it can initially repair itself forming secondary dentine which is often visible in teeth from archaeological sites. The site of caries has varied throughout the ages. In modern populations the molars and premolars are most commonly affected and the lesions occur most commonly in the fissures of these teeth or on proximal surfaces. This pattern of caries dates from the widespread introduction of sugar into the diet. It is becoming less common now following the fluoridation of drinking water and the use of fluoride toothpaste. In the past, root surface caries, often occurring at the cement-enamel junction, was the most common form. Caries is uncommon in human remains from Palaeolithic, Mesolithic, Neolithic, Bronze Age and Iron Age sites, but increases in frequency in later periods reaching its peak in modern times. Parallel to the increase in frequency, the number of teeth affected per individual has increased and so has the number of children with the disease.[1]

In America the introduction of maize caused a great increase in the rate of caries. Hunter-gatherers with a diet consisting of meat and plant food with a low carbohydrate content had low rates of caries, but when starch rich maize became the staple, caries became much more common. The lesions were predominantly on the root surface or at the cement-enamel junction, but when sugar was introduced, fissure or approximal caries became dominant, especially in children.

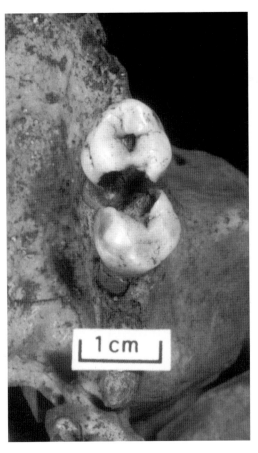

Dental abscess

Following dental caries, the pulp cavity of the tooth may become infected, and if the infection passes down the root canal an abscess is formed around the root apex. Pus may form around the apex and the pressure caused by the accumulation of pus and granulomatous tissue can be extremely painful. The abscess will eventually burst through the bone and gum, forming a fistula, or discharge into the maxillary sinus where the relief felt from the discharge of the pus may be tempered later by the development of chronic sinusitis. Dental abscesses are commonly seen in archaeological material and changes in the maxillary sinus can be seen radiologically, by direct observation when the skull is damaged, or by the use of fibre optics.

Calculus

40 Teeth from post-medieval individual from London showing massive interproximal caries. Courtesy of Dr Simon Hillson

Calculus is formed by the mineralisation of dental plaque and it may assume epic proportions in the mouths of some of our ancestors. Two kinds of calculus are distinguished, depending on whether it is above or below the gum line. Supra-gingival calculus forms on the crown and is the more common form; sub-gingival calculus forms on the surface of the roots as the gums recede in the wake of periodontal disease. In life calculus is firmly attached to the surface of the tooth, but after death it may become loose and fall off; this process is hastened considerably by taking a toothbrush to the teeth of a skeleton in the attempt to clean the teeth prior to examination. The use of any stiff brush on the teeth or on the skeleton is bound to cause friction, with resultant injury both to the specimen and the BS's temper.

Under the scanning electron microscope the remains of bacteria can be seen in calculus and an extraordinary array of materials can be incorporated into it. For example, pollen grains, fragments of plant remains and animal hairs have all been observed in calculus from British prehistoric human remains.[2] To what extent the typical diet of an individual could be inferred from the detritus in his calculus, however, remains to be seen.

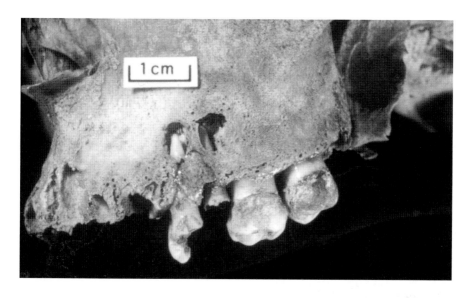

41 Mandible showing massive caries, alveolar disease, calculus and apical abscesses. Courtesy of
Dr Simon Hillson

Theoretically there is an inverse relationship between the presence of calculus and the
presence of caries. Caries results when the surface of the tooth is demineralised, whereas
the production of calculus depends upon mineralisation; the two processes are
incompatible. In practice, caries and calculus can be found in the same teeth although the
extension of the caries will be halted by the protective effect of the overlying calculus.

Periodontal disease

The periodontal tissues surround and support the teeth and they are subject to
inflammation caused by the development of an immune response to bacteria in plaque. In
human remains, periodontal disease is recognised by the loss of bone surrounding the
teeth. Two types of bone loss are described: horizontal, in which the height of all the bone
surrounding the teeth is lost simultaneously, and vertical loss which is localised around
individual teeth, leaving little ramparts of bone standing between the teeth. The loss of
bone may be substantial and is frequently associated with ante-mortem tooth loss.

Ante-mortem tooth loss

Teeth are commonly lost from the jaws both before and after death. Post-mortem tooth
loss is easily recognised as the socket shows no sign of remodelling or disease. Sometimes
loose teeth are found in the assemblage which can be replaced in the sockets. When teeth
are lost ante-mortem, the bone remodels and eventually there will be no trace at all of the

socket. The time at which a tooth was lost can be estimated — admittedly within wide limits — by the stage that the remodelling was reached.

Why teeth were lost during life may not immediately be evident, but may include trauma, primary dental disease, periodontal disease, dentistry and some systemic conditions such as scurvy. Where tooth loss occurs in the presence of widespread dental or alveolar disease, trauma is less likely to be the cause. Conversely, in a young adult, the loss of teeth was more likely to have been a fist in the mouth than most other causes. Whether ante-mortem tooth loss was the work of primitive dentists is a matter for speculation; the pain from a dental abscess can be so severe that the afflicted individual might well have consulted the village blacksmith for his assistance in removing the offending tooth. Unfortunately there does not seem to be any reliable way to determine whether or not a tooth was removed deliberately although it would be most interesting to know what the extent of dental practice was in the past and how it developed over the years.

The diagnosis of tooth loss as a concomitant of other diseases depends upon finding confirmatory evidence elsewhere in the skeleton. There are not many diseases in which tooth loss is a feature — leprosy has already been referred to and in a typical case would present no great difficulty in diagnosis. A much more common cause of tooth loss would have been scurvy, which we assume was a substantial cause of morbidity, especially in the winter months when vegetables were scarce. Although a method has recently been proposed for the diagnosis of scurvy in the skeleton, it does not seem to have any clinical basis and has yet to be validated, and it would require a great leap of faith to ascribe tooth loss to scurvy with any certainty.[3]

Dental wear

The teeth may become abraded by contact with hard materials in the food, with foreign objects such as toothpicks, or through the vigorous use of a stiff toothbrush, and is recognised by the loss of surface detail on the teeth. Attrition, which is much more common in human remains, is caused by the grinding action of the occlusal surfaces of the teeth on each other and is greatly exaggerated when the diet contains abrasive materials. The ancient Egyptian bread was thought to contain sand blown in from the desert and teeth from Egyptian contexts show extremes of attrition. There are other factors which are important in producing dental wear; grinding the teeth together — bruxism — produces more force than is exerted during chewing and may contribute to wear in some instances. Some studies have shown a relationship between the shape of the tempero-mandibular joint and tooth wear, but to my knowledge this is not something which has been studied in detail in past populations.

Tooth wear is used as an ageing criterion for both human and animal remains, and many different schemes have been proposed, some of which seem unnecessarily complicated. For use with human remains, the systems proposed by Miles and Brothwell[4] are in the most frequent use, despite their now venerable age, and they have proved to be reliable in ageing skeletons of known age.

Microwear

With the aid of the electron microscope, pits and scratches can be seen on the surface of the teeth and patterns of microwear have been used to reconstruct ancient diets. More frequent pitting, larger pits and wider scratches as taken to indicate an abrasive diet and changes which have been found in different populations are considered to have occurred following the introduction of maize in the Americas or during the intensification of agriculture during the Neolithic in the Middle East. The pattern of microwear changes rapidly during life, however, and where the diet was seasonal, all that may be reflected by the pattern of microwear is the food eaten shortly before death.

Mutilation of teeth

Deliberate mutilation of the teeth has been practised for thousands of years. Romero has provided a detailed account of the patterns which he found in the anterior teeth of early American populations. Filing, cutting and drilling were all employed to modify the teeth and Romero's classification includes no less than 69 types of mutilation.[5] Most of the modifications must have been at the very least uncomfortable and probably downright painful, and they are a good example of what people will submit to in order to conform to social mores.

Occupational and other wear

Grooves on the buccal surface of the molar teeth are common and may be the result of using tooth picks or of using the teeth as tools. In several cultures — the Inuit and the Australian aborigines, for example — animal skins or tendons are chewed to make them malleable and this may leave marks on the teeth and so may chewing plant fibres to soften them before cooking. The presence of these grooves can be taken as evidence that the teeth were used for some occupational purpose even though it may not be possible to state exactly what purpose this was.

A variety of other wear patterns may be found on the anterior teeth. Some are related to the habit of wearing stone or metal ornaments around the lips, not a common practice in Europe. A much more mundane form of dental wear is the so-called clay pipe facet. This is a circular defect frequently involving the upper and lower canines and pre-molars and invariably on one side of the mouth and it arises from years of chewing on the stem of a clay pipe.

Enamel hypoplasia

The normal enamel surface of a tooth is smooth, shiny and white, but under some circumstances the normal laying down of the enamel is interrupted and defects may appear which can be readily seen with the naked eye. The hypoplastic enamel is thinner than normal and the result is what is referred to as enamel hypoplasia. It is most readily noted on the anterior teeth and there may be several bands on a single tooth.

Enamel hypoplasia is one of a group of four conditions which many BS call stress markers, the others being cribra orbitalia, periostitis and Harris's lines, and there is a great industry in enumerating them among different populations and deriving much information about nutritional status, the prevalence of anaemia, whether a group was mobile or sedentary, the prevalence and timing of childhood diseases and so on. Often it is not entirely clear what a particular BS means by the word 'stress' and it seems to be very much a Humpty Dumpty word which can mean whatever it is wanted to mean at the time. Precise definition of terms is not a trait for which BS are especially noted. What one knows for certain about enamel hypoplasia is that it represents a period during the life of an individual when — for whatever reason — he stopped laying down enamel, and by following the pattern of hypoplasia over different teeth, the age at which this happened can be determined fairly accurately. Acute infections in children are a likely cause of enamel hypoplasia but there are many others, and children present the dentist nowadays with lesions for which there appears to be no obvious cause.

13 Chemical analysis

Bone is a composite structure consisting of hydroxy-apatite crystals in a matrix of collagen fibres. The major elements within the hydroxy-apatite crystals are calcium and phosphorus, but many other elements may either replace calcium in the crystal or attach to the surfaces of the crystal. The concentration of these elements in the skeleton varies widely and there may be differences in concentration from bone to bone, and even within the various bones themselves, but the average concentrations are shown in **Table 16**. In addition to collagen, the inorganic matrix of bone includes a number of proteins, some specific to bone such as osteocalcin, and others which are plasma proteins, including albumen and immunoglobulins. Chemical analysis of bone has concentrated on determining exposure to toxic elements and on trying to reconstruct an ancient diet.

Exposure to toxic elements

Although there are a number of toxic elements only two would have posed a risk to populations in antiquity — lead and mercury. Lead exposure arose from its use in glazes on pottery vessels used to store or cook food, and it was also used widely from the time of the Romans onwards to improve a poor wine. Its use in wine was due to the fact that when the metal was added, lead acetate was formed which has a slightly sweet taste, hence its common name, sugar of lead. The practice of adulterating wine resulted in some widespread outbreaks of lead poisoning, and the incorporation of lead into the apparatus used to crush cider apples in Devon was the cause of an endemic form of lead poisoning known in the eighteenth century as the Devonshire Colic.

The lead mines in antiquity were exploited originally to extract silver. The lead ore which was taken from the mines was galena — lead sulphide — which contains a small amount of silver. Galena is not very toxic because it is not soluble in body fluids but the process whereby silver was extracted from galena was one of the most dangerous industrial processes ever; the ore was crushed and heated to form lead oxide which was removed leaving the silver behind. Lead oxide is extremely toxic and the morbidity and mortality must have been considerable.

The mercury mines of antiquity, by contrast, would have been very dangerous places as concentrations of mercury vapour would have been high, but exposure to the general population would not have been great because mercury was not widely used. One of its principal uses was for gilding: an amalgam of mercury and gold was made and painted on

Table 16 Concentration of trace elements in bone. Essential elements are shown in italics, toxic elements in **bold**. Data from several sources

Concentration (ppm dry weight)	Elements
0-	**arsenic**, barium, **cadmium**, *cobalt*, **thallium**, *iodine*, *manganese*, **mercury**, *selenium*, silver, **tin**
1-	aluminium, *copper*, gold, *molybdenum*, *nickel*, *vanadium*
10-	boron, *chromium*, **lead**, *zinc*
100-	*flourine*, *iron*, strontium

the object to be gilded, and heated gently to drive off the mercury, leaving the gold behind. There is no doubt that this process would be likely to induce mercury poisoning in those who continued it for any length of time.

From **Table 16** it can be seen that the concentration of mercury in bone is extremely low and probably on this account it has seldom been determined in human remains. It might be interesting, however, to test the bones from monastic sites to see which of the monks might have been engaged in gilding manuscripts or to see whether individuals with syphilis from eighteenth-century cemeteries had been treated with mercury.

The situation with lead is quite the opposite. Lead is stored preferentially in the skeleton and at least 95% of the total amount of lead in the body is found there, with the concentration in the bones increasing with age. The bone lead concentration is a function of exposure and one can say that the higher the bone lead concentration, the greater the exposure during life — with one very important proviso which I will mention later.

Hundreds of papers have been published reporting the results of bone lead analysis, and this was my own first foray into the study of human remains. Having had an interest in lead poisoning in modern populations, some colleagues and I started to analyse bones from archaeological sites to determine how present day lead exposure compared with that of past populations. We analysed many hundred of samples, the largest number coming from the Romano-British site of Poundbury in Dorset. We found that bone lead levels were higher in males than in females, and that there was an increase with age — exactly as we would have predicted — and that concentrations were higher than in the modern population (**42**). When we examined the results from infants and juveniles, however, we noted a considerable anomaly; there was almost no difference in bone lead concentration at any age, and babies appeared to have been born with extremely high levels (**43**). This state of affairs was completely at odds of what is known of lead metabolism; infants are born with extremely low lead levels and there is a gradual rise during childhood. The foetus may be exposed to lead *in utero* from the mother's blood, and if sufficiently high, the foetus may abort; indeed lead compounds were quite widely used as abortifacients at one time. It is inconceivable, however, that *all* the very young infants at Poundbury were

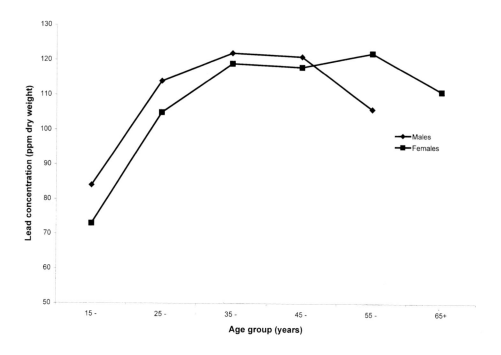

42 Bone lead concentrations by age and sex in skeletons excavated from the Romano-British cemetery at Poundbury

still born, and the most plausible explanation is that the bones had become contaminated by lead in the soil.

When we began our lead analyses we had formed the view that lead was not very mobile in the soil; the accepted wisdom was that it was firmly bound to humic acids in the soil and moved only under acid conditions. We were confident that the bone concentrations we found would be a reasonable reflection of those pertaining during life. Bones from lead coffins were found to have enormously high lead concentrations — up to 14,000 parts per million at Poundbury — and we then obtained a result which threw all our results into doubt. Some bones from Bordesley Abbey in Worcestershire were found to have a mean lead concentration of 682 parts per million, a result which was biologically impossible. The soil from the site was highly contaminated with lead, and when allowance was made for this, the mean concentration fell to *c*.40 parts per million, which was entirely convincing.[1] Since that experience I have viewed all lead analyses which are not accompanied by soil lead determinations with some scepticism, and sometimes with frank disbelief.

Nevertheless, using bone lead concentrations which can be relied on and some documentary sources, it can be shown that lead exposure has increased over the years, seeming to reach a peak in the Medieval period. The estimated relative exposure to lead at different periods is shown in **Table 17**.

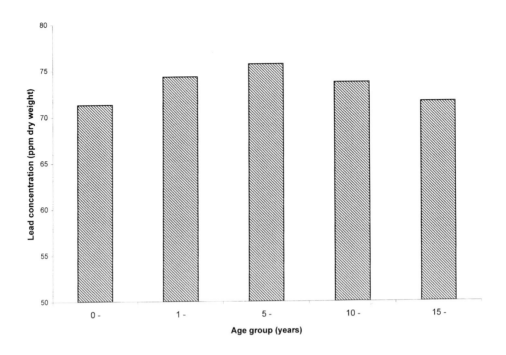

43 Bone lead concentrations in juveniles from Poundbury. There is no increase in concentration with increasing age and the most likely explanation is that the lead in the bones has come predominantly from contamination from lead in the soil

The composition of the diet

Chemical analysis has been used to determine the composition of the ancient diet based on the assumption that there is a fractionation of various elements through the food chain, and the concentration of these elements in the bones of past populations will reflect the major constituents of the diet. Trace element analysis was first employed for this purpose, but more recently the analysis of stable isotopes of carbon and nitrogen.

Trace element analysis

Three elements have been widely used to reconstruct the diet — strontium, barium and zinc. The analyses have often been used without the consideration of *a priori* requirements which must be met for the results to be valid. In order to be useful in this respect, elements should conform to the following criteria, proposed by Joseph Ezzo.[2]

- levels must be measurable in bone

- the bone levels must correlate with dietary levels

Table 17 Relative lead exposure at different periods. Lead exposure during the
Neolithic, before the advent of metal working is taken as unity

Period	Relative lead exposure
Neolithic	1.0
Iron Age	3.5
Romano-British	7.0
Medieval	13.0
Eighteenth/nineteenth century[†]	10.0
Present day[††]	4.0

[†] Based on documentary sources
[††] Based on analysis of ribs obtained at autopsy

- the fractionation from soil to diet must be known

- it must be a bone-seeking element

- it should be non-essential otherwise it will be subject to normal
  mechanisms that act to keep tissue levels constant
- it should not be very mobile in the soil

- it must have been shown possible to discriminate dietary intakes among
  modern populations using bone or tissue levels

How far any of the three most commonly used trace elements meet these criteria is
considered below.

Strontium is a non-essential, bone-seeking element which replaces calcium in the
crystal lattice. Interest in the metabolism of strontium was provoked by the atom bomb
tests during which radioactive strontium was released into the atmosphere. The gradient of
strontium in the food chain is such that levels in soil are greater than those in plants which
are, in turn, greater than those in animals. Theoretically, bones from herbivores should
contain higher levels of strontium than those of carnivores. Levels of strontium in the
modern population vary very widely, from 40-740ppm and there is no convincing evidence
that levels of strontium in bones or teeth can discriminate between different diets.

Barium behaves in a similar fashion to strontium, and strontium/barium ratios have
been said to discriminate between marine (low Ba/Sr ratios) and terrestrial (high Ba/Sr
ratios) diets. Confirmation for this from modern populations is still awaited.

Zinc is an essential element and its level is higher in meat than in plant foods. It is a
component of many metallo-enzymes in the body and also seems to be necessary for

normal growth. On the grounds of essentiality, zinc seems an inappropriate element to use for reconstructing ancient diets, and neither strontium nor barium has been shown convincingly to discriminate modern diets. None seems up to the task, therefore; analysis of stable isotopes, however, is highly promising.

Stable isotopes

Stable isotopes of elements differ in having a different number of protons in their nucleus. Their chemical properties are similar but it is found that the ratio of stable isotopes varies in different parts of the food chain and this is made use of in reconstructing ancient diets. The two stable isotopes which are most commonly used in dietary analysis are ^{13}C and ^{15}N which have an extra proton in their nucleus compared with the common forms, ^{12}C and ^{14}N. The isotopic ratio of both elements can be determined in collagen or cholesterol extracted from bone, hair and mummified tissues, and in bone mineral in the case of the carbon isotopes. The ratio in a sample is determined with reference to a standard (fossil limestone for carbon, air for nitrogen) and the ratio is expressed using a special notation (δ) which relates the ratio in the sample to that of the reference material.

In order for the inferences made from this type of analysis to be valid, it is essential to know:

• the relationship between the isotopic composition of the diet and the tissues being analyses

• the isotopic composition of the various items of the diet which are supposed to be consumed

• potential sources of variation in these relationships

• evidence that the diet of modern populations can be discriminated

The isotopic ratios of plants vary considerably according to climate (sunlight, rainfall and temperature), altitude and to partial pressures of carbon dioxide (from where they derive their carbon). These variations need to be taken into account when interpreting the results of isotopic analyses.

The technique has been extensively used in the United States and Latin America to determine the point at which maize was introduced into the economy. Maize is what is known as a C_4 plant, whereas wheat and rice are C_3 plants, where the subscript numbers refer to the number of carbon atoms in a molecule formed during the first stages of photosynthesis. C_3 plants discriminate more against $^{13}CO_2$ in the atmosphere than C_4 plants and their $\delta^{13}C$ values do not overlap; this can be made use of in determining whether or not maize was a major constituent of the diet. The technique has shown that maize was an insignificant part of the diet before about AD 1000, although it had been available in the preceding millennium. Using both carbon and nitrogen isotopes is has been possible to differentiate between marine and terrestrial diets, and the results seem both consistent and valid. The use of stable isotopes also has the great advantage that soil contamination is not a problem as it is with trace element analysis.

More recently, isotopic analysis has been applied to cholesterol extracted from archaeological bones or teeth, and this seems to be a most elegant method for reconstructing palaeodiet. The method is reproducible and the results do not vary when different bones are used a source material. Mean $\delta^{13}C$ values have been found to be lower in individuals who rely more on terrestrial foods than on marine foods (-26 compared with -22 in one study).[3] An interesting development by Richard Evershed's group has been to demonstrate that it is possible to distinguish between milk and other types of fat stored in pottery vessels since the fatty acids in milk and animal fat have characteristic $\delta^{13}C$ values.[4]

There will no doubt be further refinements of the method and we can look forward to other applications which will enable us to construct ancient menus and perhaps relate eating habits to patterns of disease.

Endpiece

This has been a guided tour rather than an exhaustive excursion, and I have deliberately limited myself to the discussion of areas that I find most interesting or about which a difference of opinion exists between different bone specialists. I hope that having arrived at the last stop, the readers will have found something to interest and inform them and that they will have formed a reasonable idea of what *can* be known from the study of human remains. This is not a text book and although the choice of references in each chapter may appear to some to be capricious or arbitrary, they will act as stepping stones to other material for those wishing to follow up particular points, and much more detail will be found in the volumes listed in the bibliography.

The study of human remains depends upon some scientific techniques and some scientific methods but it is very largely an interpretive discipline; this is both its attraction and its downfall. Scientific techniques are used for the anthropological part of the study, using measurements to determine height, weight and race; and to some extent, for assigning age and sex. Scientific methods used include *inter alia* microscopy, radiography, PCR, chemical analysis, histology and immunology. The ready availability of software packages for personal computers has led to the widespread application of statistics to bone studies sometimes without the application of a concomitant amount of thought. Statistics are still too often used as the drunk uses a lamp-post — more for support than illumination — and readers may need reminding that no amount of statistical chicanery can rescue poor data. As Austin Bradford Hill put it rather more elegantly, 'It is a serious mistake to rely upon the statistical method to eliminate disturbing factors at the completion of the work'.[1]

Using all the methods available, the BS can assign sex to adult skeletons with a high degree of reliability; using PCR sex can also be determined on juvenile skeletons, but more traditional methods are not satisfactory. Conversely, age can be determined to within close limits on juveniles but only within wide limits on adults; there is not much prospect that this state of affairs will improve in the immediate future. The height of the skeleton can be estimated using the maximum length of the long bones and trends over time can be mapped out. There are difficulties even with this apparently simple technique, and some form of standard practice would be desirable; using femoral length on its own would be as informative as calculating height and free the method from some of its unreliability. Body weight can also be estimated from bone measurements, and changes from one population to another could be determined and perhaps related to some disease states. Unless there is a particular need to estimate body habitus, as much information could be obtained by comparing the measurements which form the basis of the regression equations used in the calculation of height. The suggestion could at least be tested.

Form and shape are important for physical anthropologists who study human remains, and they have many and varied interests including the determination of race from cranial measurements, for example. This is a matter of some importance when tracing the timing and pattern of migration of peoples; in some parts of the world determination of race has important forensic implications. The form and function of bones and how they react under different stresses is also part of the physical anthropologists' remit and they have produced much important information on these points.

Age and sex determination allows the BS to construct the population profile of the assemblages they examine but there is always a considerable proportion of the assemblage to which either age or sex cannot be given, and the large number of juveniles cannot be allocated a sex. This introduces a distortion into the apparent age and sex distribution and there is a need to develop a means to overcome this; one attempt is described here which is in the process of being refined further. Attempts to derive estimates of life expectancy for skeletal assemblages are doomed to failure given the poor quality of the age at death determinations.

Chemical analysis is an area in which considerable advances are being made and is certain to become increasingly important to the study of human remains in the future. The most interesting development has been the ability to extract and analyse inorganic molecules from ancient bone. Many normal plasma and bone proteins have been extracted and at least one abnormal one; ancient DNA, genomic, mitochondrial and bacterial has been extracted and characterised using PCR, and stable isotopic analysis of collagen or cholesterol is providing information on the constituents of the diet. It is certain that in the near future more organic compounds will be extracted, perhaps rheumatoid factor or some of the HLA complex, and that the aDNA of other infectious agents, including perhaps some of the DNA viruses — hepatitis B, perhaps — will enable more accurate estimates to be made of the prevalence of some diseases and also help confirm the diagnosis of others.

Epidemiological methods can be used in the study of past populations although they have a much more limited application than in the study of modern groups. Nevertheless population studies can provide a better account of life in the past than the concentration on single cases, no matter how fascinating they may be. Using epidemiological methods the prevalence of disease in the past can be determined and changes can be recognised in the prevalence over time. Other disease rates *cannot* be calculated for past populations and BS who report on the incidence of disease, or on the infant mortality rate or the stillbirth rate, are in error; with respect to incidence, the error is probably one of nomenclature and in almost all cases in which incidence has been reported, the term is used incorrectly for prevalence. One problem in palaeoepidemiology is that of consistent diagnosis. There are very few diseases which affect the skeleton and in which the appearances are so characteristic that they cannot be misdiagnosed and it is clear that there is much inconsistency between BS in making diagnoses. This greatly limits the ability to carry out inter-study comparisons, and opportunities for such comparisons are being wasted. There is an urgent need to arrive at some agreement between BS on the development of diagnostic criteria for the common diseases which affect the skeleton. To date none has been universally agreed so there is a long way to go.

There is also scope for hypothesis testing using case-control studies but unfortunately the opportunities for this are limited because of what might be called directional problems. The BS stands at the effect end of aetiological processes rather than at the cause end, and there is no possibility of carrying out prospective studies or follow-up studies. Nor is there an opportunity of interrogating the subjects of epidemiological research or of finding out anything but the most elementary information about them, their lifestyle, habits or occupation.

When one comes to the diagnosis of disease on assessment of morbidity, and divining occupation from the skeleton, then one is setting foot very firmly across the interpretive threshold. Bone specialists must base their diagnosis on very limited information; there is not much else to go on apart from the look of the thing, perhaps an x-ray and, in a few cases, on the extraction of aDNA of abnormal proteins from the diseased bone. Modern physicians can take a personal history, a past medical history, family history, occupational history, details of symptoms and their onset, and can arrange for blood tests, x-rays, scans and any number of other diagnostic tests; from these sources they have the opportunity of seeing the disease evolve over time. And still they do not diagnose correctly in more than half to three-quarters of their patients. What hope for the BS, then? Only where there are pathognomonic signs can he be secure in the diagnosis. But, as one eminent BS once said to me, there *must* be a cause of the changes seen in the skeleton. And so there must, but what is equally certain in that we will never be able to find it in any but the most obvious cases. It is the pressure to find causes that pushes many BS into making diagnoses on the basis of flimsy evidence, often without any clinical basis. There are several palaeopathological diagnoses in the literature based on signs for which there is no clinical equivalent, and while one must recognise that some diseases might have been expressed in a form different from that today, if the appearances cannot be equated to some recognised clinical form, it is reckless to make a definite diagnosis.

There are some instances where one can be reasonably sure how an individual may have been affected by his or her disease, but they are by far the minority. Consider, for example, the description of the last days of John Torrington, one of those on Franklin's last expedition and whose body was recovered from King William Island and who was assumed to have died from lead poisoning.

It was a slow-moving and lingering illness. The early symptoms of the deadly combination of emphysema and tuberculosis with lead poisoning would have included loss of appetite, lack of concentration, shortness of breath and fatigue . . . The lack of any bed sores . . . shows that . . . on the advice of the ship's physician Torrington would have taken slow walks below decks several times a day. . . . his weight would have continued slowly dropping to the point of malnutrition. Then . . . he developed pneumonia, a serious blow to his already diminished state of health.[2]

Overlooking the diagnosis of lead poisoning about which there must be considerable doubt, a modern physician would be pleased to elicit all these symptoms from his patient, and to suggest that events would have proceeded as described is stretching credulity beyond anything reasonable. A good story, perhaps, but as a record of what actually happened — I don't think so.

Even when the appearances are extremely florid it is by no means certain that the individual was incapacitated by them during life or even knew of their presence. The changes in the spine in DISH are such that it is hard to believe that they are almost without effect. By contrast a small area of eburnation in the medial compartment of the knee may have been exquisitely painful. I once examined some femoral heads which had been surgically removed for hip replacement and been reduced to the bare bones. Some had only minimal changes and one appeared perfectly normal, it would certainly have been passed normal by any BS. My colleague Juliet Rogers likes to show a pelvic radiograph which shows one normal hip and one with joint space narrowing and much marginal osteophyte. Of course, the patient was complaining of pain in the normal looking hip; the apparently diseased hip was causing him no trouble at all.

Despite the weight of clinical evidence, BS continue to describe the symptoms experienced by their subjects and I doubt that there is any way of stopping them. They will also no doubt continue to give accounts of morbidity and adaptations to lifestyle, all gleaned from skeletal morphology with none of the benefits that one would need in order to do the same thing with the living.

What lets down the interpretive school of bone studies is that there is no means of validating the suppositions which are made. It may very well be that an attribution of occupation is correct — although the chances are extremely slim — but it will be correct for the wrong reasons and not because it has been verified. Perhaps the individual whose skeleton shows that there are several healed fractures did use a crutch; the holes in the carpal bones may be the unusual expression of rheumatoid arthritis; the individual with osteoarthritis of the hip may have suffered excruciating pain. Unfortunately, in none of these cases can one ever be *certain*; in much of their business — perhaps in *most* of their business — BS can deal only in probabilities not in certainties. It is a distressing to have to admit this but there is simply no way round in the majority of instances. In the face of certainty, the question to be asked is, 'How have you been able to validate this assumption?

Where is your proof?' And there is unlikely to be any convincing answer. There is no shame in not knowing and only when we admit that we don't know, will we try to think up means by which we may be able to know in the future.

> 'The trouble with people is not that they don't know,
> but that they know so much that ain't so.'[3]

Notes

Introduction

[1] Ötzi has just been thawed for a few hours (September 2000) so that he can be subjected to further tests; once again, the demand for samples was enormous.

[2] S. Jarcho, 'The development and present condition of human palaeopathology in the United States' in *Human Palaeopathology* (S. Jarcho ed), Yale University Press, New Haven, 1966, p5.

[3] J. Jones, *Explanation of the Aboriginal Remains in Tennessee*, Smithsonian Institution, Washington, 1876.

[4] G. Elliot Smith and F. Wood Jones, *The Archaeological Survey of Nubia 1907-8. Volume 2. Report on the Human Remains*, National Printing Department, Cairo, 1910.

[5] H.A. Waldron, 'The study of the human remains from Nubia: the contribution of Grafton Elliot Smith and his colleagues to palaeopathology', *Medical History*, 2000, 44, 363-388.

[6] C. Wells, *Bones, Bodies and Disease*, Thames and Hudson, London, 1964.

Chapter 1

[1] One of those still widely used is now 60 years old: I. Schour and M. Massler, 'The development of the human dentition', *Journal of the American Dental Association*, 1941, 28, 1153-1160. A more modern version is to be found in: D. Ferembach, I. Schwidetzky and M. Stloukal, 'Recommendations for age and sex diagnosis of skeletons', *Journal of Human Evolution*, 1980, 9, 517-549.

[2] One chart of fusion times is in D.R. Brothwell, *Digging up Bones*, British Museum, London, 1981.

[3] One set of data which is most frequently used was published by M.M. Maresh, 'Linear growth in long bones of extremities from infancy through adolescence', *American Journal of the Diseases of Children*, 1955, 89, 725-742.

[4] H. Goode, T. Waldron and J. Rogers, 'Bone growth in juveniles: a methodological noted', *International Journal of Osteoarchaeology*, 1993, 3, 321-333.

[5] See, for example, I.G. Fazekas and F. Kósa, *Forensic Fetal Osteology*, Akademia Kiado, Budapest, 1978.

[6] A dental wear chart is published by Brothwell (*Digging up Bones*, p72) and by A.E.W. Miles, 'Assessment of the ages of a population of Anglo-Saxons from their dentitions', *Proceedings of the Royal Society of Medicine*, 1962, 55, 881-886.

[7] These changes are illustrated in Brothwell (*op cit*).

[8] C.A. Kunos, S.W. Simpson, K.F. Russell and I. Hershkovitz, 'First rib metamorphosis: its possible utility for human age-at-death estimation', *American Journal of Physical Anthropology*, 1999, 110, 303-323.

[9] T. Molleson and M. Cox (eds), *The Spitalfields Project. Volume 2. The Anthropology*, Council for British Archaeology, London, 1993.

[10] L.D. Sutherland and J.M. Suchey, 'Use of the ventral arch in pubic sex determination', *Journal of Forensic Sciences*, 1991, 36, 501-511.

[11] A.C. Stone, G.R. Milner, S. Pääbo and M. Stoncking, 'Sex determination of ancient skeletons using DNA', *American Journal of Physical Anthropology*, 1996, 99, 231-238.

[12] T. Waldron, G.M. Taylor and D. Rudling, 'Sexing of Romano-British baby burials from the Bedlingham and Bignor villas', *Sussex Archaeological Collections*, 1999, 137, 71-79.

Chapter 2

[1] M. Trotter and G. Gleser, 'A re-evaluation of estimation of stature based on measurements of stature taken during life and of long bones after death', *American Journal of Physical Anthropology*, 1958, 16, 79-123; M. Trotter, 'Estimation of stature from intact limb bones' in *Personal Identification in Mass Disasters* (T.D. Stewart ed), Smithsonian Institution Press, Washington, 1970, pp 71-97.

[2] Data taken from T. Waldron, 'A note on the estimation of height from long-bone measurements', *International Journal of Osteoarchaeology*, 1998, 8, 75-77.

[3] Bennike, P., *Palaeopathology of Danish Skeletons*, Akademisk Forlag, Copenhagen, 1985.

[4] A.M.W. Porter, *Physique and the Skeleton*, PhD Thesis, University of London, 1996.

[5] Inter-Departmental Committee on Physical Deterioration, *Report, Cd 2175*, HMSO, London, 1904.

[6] The increase in height observed in Britain has been noted elsewhere. See for example D.Z. Loesch, K. Stokes and R.M. Huggins, 'Secular trend in body height and weight of Australian children and adolescents', *American Journal of Physical Anthropology*, 2000, 111, 545-556. In Japan, mean male height has apparently increased by 6cm in a single generation (K. Katayama, personal communication).

[7] Goode et al, *op cit*.

[8] I am grateful to Dr Juliet Rogers for giving me details of her unpublished results from Barton.

[9] J.M. Tanner, *A History of the Study of Human Growth*, Cambridge University Press, Cambridge, 1981.

[10] H.M. McHenry and C. Berger, 'Body proportions in *Australopithecus afarensis* and in *A. africanus* and the origin of the genus *Homo*', *Journal of Human Evolution*, 1998, 35, 1-22.

[11] A.M.W. Porter, 'An interpretation of the Boxgrove tibia', *International Journal of Osteoarchaeology*, 1998, 8, 7-10.

[12] M.B. Roberts, C.B. Stringer and S.A. Parfitt, 'A hominid tibia from middle Pleistocene sediments at Boxgrove, UK', *Nature*, 1994, 369, 311-313.

[13] E.P. Visser, 'Little waifs: estimating child body size from historic skeletal material', *International Journal of Osteoarchaeology*, 1998, 8, 413-423.

Chapter 3

[1] P. Croft, D. Coggon, M. Cruddas and C. Cooper, 'Osteoarthritis of the hip: an occupational disease in farmers', *British Medical Journal*, 1992, 304, 1269-1272.

[2] F.M. Cicuttini and T.D. Spector, 'What is the evidence that osteoarthritis is genetically determined?', *Baillieres Clinical Rheumatology*, 1997, 11, 657-669.

[3] D.T. Felson, 'Weight and osteoarthritis', *Journal of Rheumatology Supplement*, 1995, 43, 7-9.

[4] From *The Boscombe Valley Mystery*.

[5] C.F. Merbs, *Patterns of Activity-induced Pathology in a Canadian Inuit Population*, National Museums of Canada, Ottawa, 1983.

[6] N.M. Hadler, D.B. Gillings, H.R. Imbus, P.M. Levitin, D. Makuc and P.D. Utsinger, 'Hand structure and function in an industrial setting. Influence of three patterns of stereotyped repetitive usage', *Arthritis and Rheumatism*, 1978, 21, 10-20.

[7] For further details of this study, see H.A. Waldron and M. Cox, 'Occupational arthropathy: evidence from the past', *British Journal of Industrial Medicine*, 1989, 46, 420-2.

[8] C. Wells, 'Weaver, tinker or shoemaker?', *Medical and Biological Illustration*, 1967, 17, 39-47.

[9] I am very grateful to Dr Ann Stirland for these as yet unpublished data.

Chapter 4

[1] T. Waldron, *Counting the dead. The epidemiology of skeletal populations*, John Wiley & Sons, 1994.

[2] *Counting the Dead*.

[3] J. Rogers and P. Dieppe, 'Is tibiofemoral osteoarthritis in the knee joint a new disease?', *Annals of the Rheumatic Diseases*, 1994, 53, 612-613; T. Waldron, 'Changes in the distribution of osteoarthritis over historical time', *International Journal of Osteoarchaeology*, 1995, 5, 385-389.

[4] For example, see A. Adebajo and P. Davis, 'Rheumatic diseases in African blacks', *Seminars in Arthritis and Rheumatism*, 1994, 24, 139-153.

[5] Data taken from table 14.1 in A. Boddington, 'From bones to population: the problem of numbers' in *Death, Decay and Destruction* (A. Boddington, A.N. Garland and R.C. Janaway eds), Manchester University Press, Manchester, 1987, pp180-97.

[6] Other, more technical problems, are dealt with by J.T. Williams, 'Life tables in palaeodemography: a methodological note', *International Journal of Osteoarchaeology*, 1992, 2, 131-138.

[7] J.-P. Bocquet-Appel and C. Masset, 'Farewell to palaeodemography', *Journal of Human Evolution*, 1982, 11, 321-333. For a rebuttal see: D.P. van Gerven and G.J. Armelagos, '"Farewell to palaeodemography?" Rumors of its death have been greatly exaggerated', *Journal of Human Evolution*, 1983, 12, 353-360.

Chapter 5

[1] G.T. Nurse and T. Jenkins, *Health and the Hunter-Gatherer: Biomedical Studies on the Hunting and Gathering Populations of Southern Africa*, Karger, Basel, 1977; R.J. Shephard, *The Health Consequences of 'Modernization': Evidence from Circumpolar Peoples*, Cambridge University Press, Cambridge, 1996.

[2] E.D. Sverdlov, 'Retroviruses and primate evolution', *Bioessays*, 2000, 22, 161-171.

[3] E. Larsson and G. Anderson, 'Beneficial role of human endogenous retroviruses: facts and hypotheses', *Scandinavian Journal of Immunology*, 1998, 48, 329-338.

Chapter 6

[1] Cattaneo, C., Gelsthorpe, K., Phillips, P., Waldron, T., Booth, J.R. and Sokol, R.J., 'Immunological diagnosis of multiple myeloma in a medieval bone', *International Journal of Osteoarchaeology*, 1994, 4, 1-2.

[2] T. Waldron, 'An unusual cluster of meningiomas?', *International Journal of Osteoarchaeology*, 1998, 8, 213-217.

[3] See, for example, T. Anderson, 'A medical example of meningiomatous hyperostosis', *British Journal of Neurosurgery*, 1991, 5, 399-404.

[4] C.J. Hackett, *Diagnostic Criteria of Syphilis, Yaws and Treponarid (*Treponematoses*) and of Some Other Diseases in Dry Bones (for use in Osteo-archaeology)*, Springer, Berlin, 1976.

Chapter 7

[1] M. Cox, T. Molleson and T. Waldron, 'Preconceptions and perception: the lesson of a nineteenth-century suicide', *Journal of Archaeological Science*, 1990, 17, 573-581.

[2] J. Bowman, S.M. MacLaughlin and J.L. Scheuer, 'Burial of an early nineteenth-century suicide in the crypt of St Bride's Church, Fleet Street', *International Journal of Osteoarchaeology*, 1992, 2, 91-94.

[3] M. Harman, T.I. Molleson and J.L. Price, 'Burials, bodies and beheadings in Romano-British and Anglo-Saxon burials', *Bulletin of the British Museum of Natural History (Geology)*, 1981, 35, 145-88.

[4] F. Wood Jones, 'The examination of the bodies of 100 men executed in Nubia in Roman times', *British Medical Journal*, 1908i, 736.

[5] V. Vermooten, 'A study of the fracture of the epistropheus due to hanging with a note on the possible causes of death', *Anatomical Record*, 1921, 20, 305-311.

[6] R. James and R. Nasmyth-Jones, 'The occurrence of cervical fractures in victims of judicial hanging', *Forensic Science International*, 1992, 54, 81-91.

[7] The previous year, a human skull had been found which was handed to the police. The skull was apparently that of a young woman and suspicion fell on a man who had confessed to his cell mate that he had murdered his wife. On being told of the finding of the skull, he confessed to, and was later convicted of the murder of his wife. Ironically, the skull was radiocarbon dated at Oxford and a date of 1740 ± 80 BP was obtained. (See, R.C. Turner, Discovery and excavation of the Lindow bodies, in I.M. Stead, J.B. Bourke and D. Brothwell (eds), *Lindow Man. The Body in the Bog*, Guild Publishing, London, 1986, p10.)

[8] P.V. Glob, *The Bog People. Iron-Age Man Preserved*, Faber and Faber, London, 1969.

[9] T.D. White, *Prehistoric Cannibalism at Mancos 5MTUMR-2346*, Princeton University Press, Princeton, 1992.

[10] T.D. White, *Prehistoric Cannibalism at Mancos 5MTUMR-2346*, Princeton University Press, Princeton, 1992.

[11] C.G. Turner II and J.A. Turner, *Man Corn. Cannibalism and Violence in the Prehistoric American Southwest*, University of Utah Press, Salt Lake City, 1999.

[12] M.D. Ogilvie and C.E. Hilton, 'Ritualized violence in the prehistoric American Southwest', *International Journal of Osteoarchaeology*, 2000, 10, 27-48.

Chapter 8

[1] J. Rogers and T. Waldron, *A Field Guide to Joint Disease on Archaeology*, John Wiley & Son, Chichester, 1995.

[2] J. Rogers and P. Dieppe, 'Is tibiofemoral osteoarthritis in the knee joint a new disease?', *Annals of the Rheumatic Diseases*, 1994, 53, 612-613; T. Waldron, 'Changes in the distribution of osteoarthritis over historical time', *International Journal of Osteoarchaeology*, 1995, 5, 385-389.

[3] H.A. Waldron, 'Osteoarthritis of the hands in early populations', *British Journal of Rheumatology*, 1996, 35, 1292-1298.

[4] H.A. Waldron, 'Association between osteoarthritis of the hand and knee in a population of skeletons from London', *Annals of the Rheumatic Diseases*, 1997, 56, 116-118.

[5] L. Kilgore, 'Possible case of rheumatoid arthritis from Sudanese Nubia', *American Journal of Physical Anthropology*, 1989, 79, 177-183.

[6] T. Appelboom, C. de Boelpaepe, G.E. Ehrlich and J.P. Famaey, 'Rubens and the question of antiquity of rheumatoid arthritis', *Journal of the American Medical Association*, 1981, 245, 483-486.

[7] A.M. Abdel-Nasser, J.J. Rasker and H.A. Valkenburg, 'Epidemiological and clinical aspects relating to the variability of rheumatoid arthritis', *Seminars in Arthritis and Rheumatism*, 1997, 27, 123-140.

[8] Ossification of the PLL is very common in the Japanese and is a common cause of spinal cord compression requiring surgical intervention. It is rarely seen outside Japan except in association with DISH.

[9] T. Waldron, 'DISH at Merton Priory: evidence for a 'new' occupational disease?', *British Medical Journal*, 1985, 291, 1762-1763.

[10] J. Rogers and T. Waldron, 'DISH and the monastic way of life', *International Journal of Osteoarchaeology*, in the press.

[11] Barbara Harvey, *Living and Dying in England 1100-1540. The Monastic Experience*, Clarendon Press, Oxford, 1993.

[12] G.V. Ball, 'Two epidemics of gout', *Bulletin of the History of Medicine*, 1971, 45, 401-408.

Chapter 9

[1] There are some other rarer forms of tuberculosis often found in patients whose immune system has been compromised. Since these could not be expected among skeletal assemblages, I have omitted any discussion of them.

[2] D. Morse, D.R. Brothwell and P. Ucko, 'Tuberculosis in ancient Egypt', *American Review of Respiratory Diseases*, 1964, 90, 524-541.

[3] G.M. Taylor, M. Goyal, A.J. Legge, R.J. Shaw and D. Young, 'Genotypic analysis of *Mycobacterium tuberculosis* from medieval human remains', *Microbiology*, 1999, 145, 899-904.

[4] H.D. Donaghue, M. Spigelman, J. Zias, A.M. Gernaey-Child and D.E. Minnikin, '*Mycobacterium tuberculosis* complex DNA in calcified pleura from remains 1400 years old', *Letters in Applied Microbiology*, 1998, 27, 265-269.

[5] V. Møller-Christensen, 'New knowledge of leprosy through paleopathology', *International Journal of Leprosy*, 1965, 33, 603-610.

[6] There are a number of borderline types of leprosy in which the characteristics of the two main types are mixed.

[7] R. Reader, 'New evidence for the antiquity of leprosy in early Britain', *Journal of Archaeological Science*, 1974, 1, 205-207.

[8] C.J. Hackett, *Diagnostic Criteria of Syphilis, Yaws and Treponarid (*Treponematoses*) and of Some Other Diseases in Dry Bones (for use in Osteo-archaeology)*, Springer, Berlin, 1976.

[9] A. Stirland, 'The origin of syphilis. Before or after 1493?', *International Journal of Osteoarchaeology*, 1994, 4, 53-54.

Chapter 10

[1] One example is in the Hunterian Museum of the Royal College of Surgeons.

[2] G. Harley, *Native African Medicine*, Frank Cass, London, 1970; S. Webb, *Palaeopathology of Aboriginal Australians*, Cambridge University Press, Cambridge, 1995.

[3] Evidence for care in the community in past times has come from the study of other chronic conditions. See, for example, A. Stirland, 'Care in the medieval community', *International Journal of Osteoarchaeology*, 1997, 7, 587-90.

[4] W.P. Coues, Robert Liston, *Medical Life*, 1922, 29, 540-55.

[5] S. Hillson, T. Waldron, B. Owen-Smith and L. Martin, 'Benjamin Franklin, Williams Hewson and the Craven Street bones', *Archaeology International*, 1998/99, 14-16.

[6] O. Temkin, *Translation of Soranus' Gynecology*, John Hopkin's Press, Baltimore, 1956.

[7] E.R. Kerley, 'The identification of battered-infant skeletons', *Journal of Forensic Sciences*, 1978, 23, 163-168.

[8] E.L. Margetts, 'Trephanation of the skull by the medicine-man of primitive cultures, with particular reference to present-day native East African practice' in *Diseases in Antiquity* (D. Brothwell and A.T. Sandison eds), C.C. Thomas, Springfield, 1967, pp673-701.

Chapter 11

[1] *Bones, Bodies and Disease*, p73.

[2] D. Brothwell, 'The evidence for neoplasms' in *Diseases in Antiquity*, p320.

[3] T. Waldron, 'A nineteenth-century case of carcinoma of the prostate, with a note on the early history of the disease', *International Journal of Osteoarchaeology*, 1997, 7, 244-247.

[4] T. Waldron, 'What was the prevalence of malignant disease in the past?', *International Journal of Osteoarchaeology*, 1996, 6, 463-470.

Chapter 12

[1] The most comprehensive investigation of the history of caries in human remains was carried out by Jim Moore and Liz Corbett and published in three classic papers: W.J. Moore and M.E. Corbett, 'Distribution of caries in ancient British populations: I.

Anglo-Saxon period', *Caries Research*, 1971, 5, 151-168; 'II. Iron Age, Romano-British and Medieval periods', *Ibid*, 1973, 7, 139-153; 'III. The seventeenth century', *Ibid*, 1975, 9, 163-175.

[2] K. Dobney and D. Brothwell, 'Dental calculus: its relevance to ancient diet and oral ecology' in *Teeth and Anthropology* (E. Cruwys and R.A. Foley eds), BAR, Oxford, 1986, pp52-82.

[3] D.J. Ortner, E.H. Kimmerle and M. Diez, 'Probable evidence of scurvy in subadults from archaeological sites in Peru', *American Journal of Physical Anthropology*, 1999, 108, 321-331.

[4] A.E.W. Miles, 'Assessment of the ages of a population of Anglo-Saxons from their dentitions', *Proceedings of the Royal Society of Medicine*, 1962, 55, 881-886; D.R. Brothwell, *Digging up Bones*, British Museum, London, 1981.

[5] J. Romero, 'Dental mutilation, trephination and cranial deformation' in *Physical Anthropology* (T.D. Stewart ed), 1970, pp50-67.

Chapter 13

[1] The full account can be found in H.A. Waldron, 'On the post-mortem accumulation of lead by skeletal tissues', *Journal of Archaeological Science*, 1983, 10, 35-40.

[2] J.A. Ezzo, 'Putting the "chemistry" back into archaeological bone chemistry analysis: modelling potential paleodietary indicators', *Journal of Anthropological Archaeology*, 1994, 13, 1-34.

[3] A.W. Stott and R.P. Evershed, '$\delta^{13}C$ analysis of cholesterol preserved in archaeological bones and teeth', *Analytical Chemistry*, 1996, 15, 4402-4408.

[4] S.N. Dudd and R.P. Evershed, 'Direct demonstration of milk as an element in archaeological economies', *Science*, 1998, 282, 1478-1481.

Endpiece

[1] A. Bradford Hill and I.D. Hill, *Bradford Hill's Principles of Medical Statistics, 12th Edition*, Edward Arnold, London, 1991, p3.

[2] O. Beattie and J. Geiger, *Frozen in Time. The Fate of the Franklin Expedition*, Grafton Books, London, 1989, p124.

[3] *Josh Billings' Encyclopedia of Wit and Wisdom*

Bibliography

This bibliography is not intended to be a comprehensive guide to the literature about human remains but it should provide a good starting point for anyone wishing to learn more. The choice is, of course, idiosyncratic and includes some up-to-date texts, but also some classics — *Bones, Bodies and Disease, Diseases in Antiquity* and *The Evolution and Eradication of Infectious Diseases*, for example — which will only be available from libraries, and then perhaps only with difficulty. I have also included a few books simply because they are a joy to read, and one monumental reference work, which is a tribute to the industry and erudition of its authors. I make no apologies either for inclusions or omissions.

Alexander, R. McNeill, *Bones. The Unity of Form and Function*, Weidenfeld and Nicholson, London, 1994.

Arcini, C., *Health and Disease in Early Lund*, Lund University, Lund, 1999.

Bennike, P., *Palaeopathology of Danish Skeletons*, Akademisk Forlag, Copenhagen, 1985.

Boddington, A., Garland, A.N. and Janaway, R.C. (eds), *Death, Decay and Reconstruction. Approaches to Archaeology and Forensic Science*, Manchester University Press, Manchester, 1987.

Brothwell, D.R., *Digging up Bones*, British Museum, London, 1981.

Brothwell, D. and Sandison, A.T. (eds), *Diseases in Antiquity*, C.C. Thomas, Springfield, 1967.

Brothwell, D., *The Bog Man and the Archaeology of People*, British Museum Publications, London, 1986.

Cockburn, A., *The Evolution and Eradication of Infectious Diseases*, Johns Hopkins Press, Baltimore, 1963.

Cockburn, A., Cockburn, E. and Reyman, T.A. (eds), *Mummies, Disease & Ancient Cultures*, 2nd edition, Cambridge University Press, Cambridge, 1998.

Cox, M. and Mays, S. (eds), *Human Osteology in Archaeology and Forensic Science*, Greenwich Medical Media, London, 2000.

Dutour, O. and Pálfi, G. (eds), *L'origine de la syphilis en Europe: avant ou après 1493?*, Editions Errance, Paris, 1994.

Fairgrieve, S.I. (ed), *Forensic Osteological Analysis*, C.C. Thomas, Springfield, 1999.

Feinnes, R.N.T.W., *Zoonoses and the Origins and Ecology of Human Disease*, Academic Press, London, 1978.

Hillson, S.W., *Dental Anthropology*, Cambridge University Press, Cambridge, 1996.

Hoppa, R.D. and FitzGerald, C.M. (eds), *Human Growth in the Past: Studies from Bones and Teeth*, Cambridge University Press, Cambridge, 1999.

Jurmain, R. (ed), *Essentials of Physical Anthropology*, Wadsworth, London, 1998.

Katzenberg, M.A. and Saunders, S.R. (eds), *Biological Anthropology of the Human Skeleton*, Wiley-Liss, New York, 2000.

Krogman, W.M. and Isçan, M.Y., *The Human Skeleton in Forensic Medicine*, C.C. Thomas, Springfield, 1986.

Larsen, C.L., *Interpreting Behaviour from the Human Skeleton*, Cambridge University Press, Cambridge, 1999.

Martin, D.L. and Frayer, D.W. (eds), *Troubled Times. Violence and Warfare in the Past*, Gordon and Breach, Amsterdam, 1997.

Merbs, C.F., *Patterns of Activity-induced Pathology in a Canadian Inuit Population*, National Museums of Canada, Ottowa, 1983.

Ortner, D. and Aufderheide, A.C. (eds), *Identification of Pathological Conditions in Human Skeletal Remains*, Smithsonian Institution, Washington, 1981.

Pálfi, G., Dutour, O., Deák, and Hutás, I. (eds), *Tuberculosis Past and Present*, Golden Book Publisher, 1999.

Reichs, K.J., *Forensic Osteology. Advances in the Identification of Human Remains*, C.C. Thomas, Springfield, 1997.

Resnick, D. and Niwayama, G., *Diagnosis of Bone and Joint Disorders*, W.B. Saunders, Philadelphia, 1988.

Roberts, C. and Manchester, K. *The Archaeology of Disease*, 2nd edition, Sutton Publishing, Stroud, 1996.

Rogers, J. and Waldron, T., *A Field Guide to Joint Disease in Archaeology*, John Wiley & Sons, Chichester, 1995.

Sandford, M.K. (ed), *Investigations of Ancient Human Tissue: Chemical Analyses in Anthropology*, Gordon and Breach, Philadelphia, 1993.

Scheuer, L. and Black, S., *Developmental Juvenile Osteology*, Academic Press, London, 2000.

Stein, P.L. and Rowe, B.M., *Physical Anthropology*, McGraw-Hill, Boston, 2000.

Stirland, A., *Human Bones in Archaeology*, Shire, Princes Risborough, 1999.

Ubelaker, D.H., *Human Skeletal Remains: Excavation, Analysis, Interpretation*, Taraxacum, Washington, 1989.

Waldron, T., *Counting the Dead. The Epidemiology of Skeletal Populations*, John Wiley & Sons, Chichester, 1994.

Wells, C., *Bones, Bodies and Disease*, Thames and Hudson, London, 1964.

White, T.D., *Human Osteology*, Academic Press, London, 1991.

Index